LINCOLN
IN SPRINGFIELD

For Asher —
in thanks for his
interest in my Lincoln

Jan Jacobi

books!

All the best,
Jan Jacobi
1-14-2022

Library of Congress Control Number: 2021935147

ISBN: 9781681063256

Printed in the United States of America
21 22 23 24 25   5 4 3 2 1

DEDICATION

Abraham Lincoln loved cats.
This book is dedicated to our cat, Dunny,
who sat with me as I wrote it, and died on
March 21, 2020, before it was finished.

TABLE OF CONTENTS

PREFACE

By the way, a fine example was presented on board the boat for contemplating the effect of condition upon human happiness. A gentleman had purchased twelve negroes in different parts of Kentucky and was taking them to a farm in the South. They were chained six and six together. A small iron clevis was around the left wrist of each, and this fastened to the main chain by a shorter one at a convenient distance from, the others; so that the negroes were strung together precisely like so many fish upon a trot-line. In this condition they were being separated forever from the scenes of their childhood, their friends, their fathers and mothers, and brothers and sisters, and many of them, from their wives and children, and going into perpetual slavery where the lash of the master is proverbially more ruthless and unrelenting than any other where; and yet amid all these distressing circumstances, as we would think them, they were the most cheerful and apparently happy creatures on board. One, whose offence for which he had been sold was an over-fondness for his wife, played the fiddle almost continually; and the others danced, sung, cracked jokes, and played various games with cards from day to day. How true it is that "God tempers the wind to the shorn lamb," or in other words, that He renders the worst of human conditions tolerable, while He permits the best, to be nothing better than tolerable.

The preface is excerpted from a letter Lincoln wrote to Mary Speed, the half sister of his friend Joshua Speed, on September 27, 1841. Lincoln was returning to Springfield with Speed, after having spent six weeks with the Speed family on their plantation near Louisville, KY. Lincoln and Speed journeyed from Louisville to St. Louis by steamboat.

PART ONE

Chapter One

A RISING MAN

At the far end of Joshua Speed's store was an enormous fireplace. The hearthstones extended out several feet. Massive, interlocking stones, held in place with mortar, framed the firepit, and formed its back wall. Without a fire, a man might imagine that he was about to enter an inviting cave. A large blackened grate held the logs firmly as a farmer might hold a newborn lamb. When the glow from the fires of fall and winter lit the room, it brought warmth and fellowship.

To Speed's store, at one point or another, came each of the rising young men of Springfield. Speed was so likable that he became friends with them all. As they purchased groceries, a book, some medicine, or a stylish shirt, they struck up a conversation with the storekeeper. New arrivals were always welcomed at Speed's store and soon adopted into the group of friends.

Three of us, John Hardin, Stephen Douglas, and I, were representatives in the Illinois legislature. Our friend, Edward Baker, had been elected to an open seat in July. Everyone was a Whig except Douglas. He was an ardent supporter of Andrew Jackson, whom the rest of us detested. Despite our political differences, we were able to remain friends with Douglas.

On a cold night in mid-September 1837, we gathered in front of our first fire of the season. Douglas, who never sat down, was striding up and down in front of the fireplace. Baker and I lounged on barrels nearby. Reading the latest edition of the *Sangamo Journal*, Hardin stood erect by the window. Speed sprawled comfortably on the floor.

"Lincoln," crowed Douglas, "is it true that when you moved to Springfield, you rode on a borrowed horse?"

I ignored him.

Douglas was a short man with a large head surrounded by waves of black hair. Thick black brows sprouted lushly over his eyes, which were dark and shifty. He was thick set with sturdy shoulders. He strutted around like an agitated rooster.

He continued, "And did the full extent of your earthly possessions fit into your saddlebags?"

I looked away from him and said nothing.

"And did you not stuff Blackstone's *Commentary on the Laws of England* into one of those bags?" he cried as if resting his case.

"Meaning that you were dirt poor when you came to this thriving metropolis," echoed Hardin without looking up from the newspaper. He was tall, thin, and very handsome. His bearing was dignified, which suited someone whose father had been a senator from Kentucky.

"Aha!" yelled Baker who often took my side in this jousting. "Lincoln, what do you have to say for yourself?" He was handsome as well with a round face that radiated energy and passion.

I couldn't hide behind feigned indifference any longer.

"Douglas," I asked, "Is it true that when you first came here, you were so desperate for money that you rounded up a bunch of ragamuffins and attempted to teach them school? And how did this noble project fare? Did you give them lashes when they called you 'Ichabod'?"

"Aha!" cried Baker once more, "a hit, a palpable hit."

"Nothing of the sort," growled Douglas, "I learned 'em their letters and numbers and collected their fees."

"Well," I replied, "if you claim victory over the rascals, and if they learned anything, you must have beaten it into them."

"Not so, that's the usual hogwash you serve up. The boys wanted me to stay and marry one of their sisters. They were fetching lasses, but none was right for a rising man like me."

"Then is it true," I followed up, "that you failed twice as a carpenter?"

"Where are you getting this twaddle? Yes, I was indentured to my uncle who taught me carpentry, and I apprenticed with Nahum Parker, but the only cabinetmaking that interests me now is in Washington."

This set Hardin in motion. He folded the newspaper, placed it on the window shelf, and advanced toward Douglas. He looked like a long-legged bird about to spear a frog.

"You aren't the only ambitious one among us. One of us might be there before you, and find a place in the cabinet for you as a whistling tea kettle."

Hardin paused and then added, "However, I like Douglas's line of questioning. Tell us, Speed, on this day when Lincoln arrived in Springfield, did he come to your store in search of bedding?"

"Yes, he did," said Speed earnestly.

He had a pleasant face with appealing features: prominent eyebrows, blue eyes, and a well-shaped nose. The corners of his mouth turned up indicating a sunny disposition. The features united to create an expression of kindness and warmth.

"And how much did this bedding cost?"

"Seventeen dollars."

"Did he pay you for it?"

"No, he asked me to give him credit until Christmas. He said that he had come to Springfield to practice law, and that if his experiment was successful, he would be able to pay me. If it were to fail, he would not."

"How did you resolve this?"

"I told him I could suggest a plan by which he could find accommodation without incurring any debt. I have a large double bed upstairs, and I invited him to share it with me. He grabbed his saddlebags, bounded up the stairs, came down, and greeted me with a broad smile. 'Well, Speed,' he said, 'I am moved.'"

"Now, Speed, here is the question to which we all want to know the answer, 'Did he strike you as a rising man, as a man of ambition advancing rapidly through the established levels of society?'"

"Well, it may surprise you, but we talked about that."

"Indeed, what did he say?"

"It's more what I said. He came into the store and introduced himself. I told him I already knew him, and that I had seen him give a speech by the courthouse in Springfield when he was running for his second term in the legislature."

Baker interrupted excitedly, "You mean the one where he gave Forquer the slasher-gaff?"

Although Douglas would never admit it, Baker was the best orator among us. He was known for his fiery speeches. He was a master of the slasher-gaff, which was tearing an opponent to pieces with scorn and sarcasm.

"Yes," said Speed. "I was there when Forquer said he'd have to take the young man down."

"But I was too quick for him," I jumped in eagerly. "I got Forquer back with a slasher-gaff of my own and speared him with his lightning rod, so to speak."

Speed looked as pained as he did when we first spoke about this.

Baker asked him what was wrong.

"I asked Lincoln if he enjoyed being the slasher-gaff. It seemed so unlike my first sense of him."

"And what did he say?" asked Hardin.

"He should speak for himself," said Speed.

"I couldn't admit that I didn't," I answered, "and then Speed asked if I really wanted to hurt people deliberately."

"And you said?"

"I said that if they did it to me, there was no reason why I shouldn't do it back to them. I said it was like catching them on a large fishhook and watching them flap around. I enjoyed getting—"

At that moment, a piercing scream came from the street near Speed's store. We rushed toward the door, and Speed led us outside into the street.

There we encountered a frightening sight. An older man with a beefy frame had a whip in his hand and was lashing a woman who cowered down into the mud.

My companions were temporarily stunned into inaction, but I yelled at them, "Let's help her, friends. It's the shoemaker who lives next door. He's drunk and been beating his wife."

As I rallied them, I shouted, "I warned him the last time that if he ever did it again, I would give him a beating he wouldn't forget."

We stormed into the street and wrestled the man away from his wife. Douglas, who was always ready for an altercation, ripped the whip out of his hands.

Hardin and Baker grabbed hold of the man's arms, jerked him out of the mud, and lugged him to the hitching posts next to Speed's store.

Hardin yelled, "Lincoln, what do you want to do with him?"

"Speed, bring us some rope from inside. Hold him by the post, boys, until Speed comes out."

Speed emerged with a coil of thick rope, and I gave the order.

"Tie him to the post."

The shoemaker tried to kick and bite as Hardin and Baker grabbed his arms and legs. He hollered obscene threats at Baker who pushed him up against the post. I ripped the shirt off his back, and then Douglas, reveling in his task, bound the drunken man to the post. When it was done, we toppled down onto the steps in front of the store.

After we recovered, Douglas asked, "What next, Lincoln?"

"Aha, you will see!" I cried.

During the fracas, the shoemaker's wife collapsed on the ground, her clothes torn to rags by her husband's merciless lashes. She cradled her head in her arms and moaned continually.

When I advanced toward her, she backed away.

"Please," I said, "we are here to help."

As she looked up at me, I had never seen a creature so bewildered. Her face showed she was torn between fear and joy—part victim and part fair lady.

I continued to reassure her as best I could.

I reached out to help her. Reluctantly she took hold of my arm. Gradually, as I pulled her up, she regained

her footing and stood by my side. Poor soul, we rescued
her just in time.

I spoke to her in a low voice.

"We must be certain he never does it again. There is
one way." I signaled for Douglas to give me the whip. I
took it and handed it to her.

She grasped it, but at first she did not comprehend. I
held her hand and led it through the motion of giving a
lash. I did it a second and a third time. Then I pointed
to her husband.

This time she understood. With a pained expression,
she turned away and grunted,

"Oh…no…no…no…"

"But you must."

"I cannot."

"You must. If you don't, he will continue to harm
you."

A trace of anger giving way to relief rippled across her
face, the chance to avenge a lifetime of wrongs.

She stepped toward her husband and delivered a
tentative lash.

"Go to it, Ma'am!" yelled Douglas.

"Give him what he deserves!" added the hot-blooded
Baker. "Remember what he did to you."

Each of her lashes hit him a little harder. The
moans now came from her husband. Again and again,
she struck with power. The shoemaker screamed with
pain as the blood dribbled and then flowed down his
back. When the whip tore small pieces of flesh from his
wounds, I stepped in to stop it.

The shoemaker's wife stood by with a new fire lit in

her eyes. Baker and Douglas untied her husband. We put his shirt back on before he crumpled to the ground. We waited until he began to crawl home through the mud.

His wife continued to stand by the pole.

I stepped slowly toward her. The mud grabbed my boots and sucked angrily as I pulled them free. The others stood back while I approached her.

Perhaps she wanted to thank us, but she hesitated and looked away.

"You should go home," I said, "he will not harm you again."

She eyed me once more, bowed her head ever so slightly, and receded into the night.

No one spoke as Speed led us up the steps, into the store, and back to our familiar spots by the fireplace. He added several logs to the fire and stirred it slowly. The new wood crackled and spat as flames rose and curled around it. Although we began to feel its renewing warmth, we were still silent.

When we gathered, Baker was often the first to speak. He was always ready to jump into any argument or discussion.

On this evening, he did not shrink from being first. He stood up, walked to the fire, and turned to face us. We expected a pronouncement of some kind. When he did this, he thrust out his chest like a bird ruffling its feathers. At this moment, however, he seemed unusually grim.

"Why would he do that?"he asked.

No one spoke.

He asked the question again.

"Baker, that isn't the kind of question we'd expect you to ask. You've stunned us into silence," replied Hardin.

"I want to know the answer!"

"The problem," said Speed, "is that there isn't one."

"A question with no answer," said Douglas, "why should we bother with it?"

Hardin added, "Well that's a good point." Then he turned toward me to ask another question.

"Lincoln, what makes you so sure he won't beat her again?"

"He won't"

"But why not? How do you know?"

"It's obvious," chortled Douglas, "he's heard from destiny and understands the principles that govern our world."

"No, Speed is right. We will never know why he was doing it. And I do not know why he will not beat her again, but I am certain, because of what we did, he will not. We helped set her free."

Chapter Two

THE FULLNESS
OF THE PRAIRIE

Although they had been pestering me, my friends were right about the afternoon of April 15, 1837, when I arrived in Springfield, and Speed invited me to stay with him. He was so kind and congenial that I agreed at once. After I took Pumpkin to a livery stable, Speed and I enjoyed a sparse dinner, relaxed by his fireplace, and then retired to the upstairs room to sleep. Within minutes, he was snoring contentedly.

I could not sleep. It was not unexpected. I had never slept particularly well, but I was more restless than usual. I gave it an hour or two, but finally rose from the bed, dressed warmly, and climbed down the ladder to the main floor. A sliver of light from the first quarter moon lured me out the door toward the wooden platforms that served as the town's sidewalks.

Speed's store was on the northwest corner of the town square. The silhouette of the Sangamon County Courthouse rose to meet the sweep of the early spring stars. I crossed through the mud to the other side of the street. I intended to walk until I felt more settled, but when I found a bench in front of the courthouse, I decided to sit quietly and observe the night sky.

Though I knew many of the constellations, very few resembled the figure for which they were named. An exception was Leo, the resting lion, which was low in the east. His sturdy grace began to draw me out of my unease.

I let my thoughts flow, and images arose of the afternoon journey from New Salem to Springfield. Like a kaleidoscope, the images blended into each other.

It had been time for me to leave New Salem. The village was dying, but it was not easy to depart. It had been my home for six years, the only home I'd known while being on my own. I arrived there with no direction or purpose. I found friends who welcomed me and guided me. I got my start in law and politics, and I learned that by reading, I could make up for the school I had missed.

Even though I had gained confidence, moving to Springfield meant I'd be starting over again. What if I failed as a lawyer? What if I fell even deeper into debt? Where would I live? Would it be as easy to make friends as it had been in Salem? Would I find a young woman to marry? The people in Springfield were different. They were fancier than I was. Would they laugh at my country ways? Could I contend with the leading lawyers of Springfield: Baker, Douglas, Hardin, and Forquer? They were well educated and so far ahead of me.

Henry Onstot, the cooper, promised to loan me a horse for my departure. I stopped by the tavern that he still ran for the travelers who sometimes passed through. He made barely enough to keep it open. Henry said he'd give me a farewell dinner, but he also said his fixings would be pretty meager.

When we sat down at the table, he said, "It's mighty rough around here, but you know that as well as anyone. Couldn't nothin' keep you here. Most all of them are gone now, on up to Petersburg where you laid out them plats."

I told him it reminded me of the drunken farmer and his sheep. A drunken farmer had only one sheep left. All the others had wandered off to neighboring flocks. Before he went to bed, he tied up the sheep, but when he woke the next morning, it was gone. "Well, ain't that the damndest," he said, "I guess I'll have to go live where they gone."

Henry had replied, "Abe, you're far too young to be forgetful. That ain't a good thing for a politician. You told me that one last week, and once afore that. You got to keep track who you told stories to and who you ain't."

While we ate our dinner, we didn't say too much, but at the end he piped up, "You'd better take Pumpkin. She's slow, but she'll give you a steady ride. It's strange about horses. They seem to know what's on our mind. She's the one for you to take to Springfield today."

I left the tavern and saddled up Pumpkin with all the possessions I owned in the world: two saddlebags stuffed full of clothes and two heavy law books. There wasn't much else to do but get on the road to Springfield. Henry was at the tavern door, and he set me on my way before going back inside. I spoke gently to Pumpkin, gave her a slight nudge with the side of my foot, and we were on our way.

It was warmer than usual for early spring. Although the day started with sunshine, clouds were rolling in. The air hung heavy, and darker clouds, beginning to gather in the west, meant a late day thunderstorm. We'd still have time to reach Springfield ahead of the rain.

Before long, we were out in the open prairie. The road was a grass path worn down by the horses and wagons passing between New Salem and Springfield. With warmer weather had come the first clumps of green, which were trying desperately to survive the hoofprints, the wagon tracks, and the mud. Rising out from us toward the horizon were waves of light brown prairie grasses, remnants of the previous year's growth. The red butterfly weed and the white meadow lilies broke through the lower lying grasses.

Under the openness of the prairie sky, a man could feel utterly alone. I felt it, was even awed by it, but I was not uncomfortable with it. It was that way when I looked up at the stars on a night when the moon was down.

As Pumpkin and I walked, and occasionally trotted, into the fullness of the prairie, it seemed to me that it spoke of possibilities. I was going to Springfield to become a lawyer. John Todd Stuart had asked me to be his partner. I needed someone to initiate me into the ways of lawyers and the law, so I welcomed Stuart's invitation.

During my first term in the legislature in 1834, Stuart had been my mentor. I'd had to feel my way around. It was in the second term that I got the hang of it. We'd put through a program of internal improvements for Illinois, and I'd been a leader in moving the state capital from Vandalia to Springfield. I'd also learned how to take down my political opponents in discussion and debate.

Pumpkin may have sensed the coming storm. She whinnied and pawed the ground. I gave her several light pats on her neck, and she settled into a soothing walk. Whether it was the steady rhythm of her gait or the gradual clearing of my mind, I felt more relaxed.

It was best not to think too hard about what was coming and to appreciate the spring afternoon. After a hard winter, the warmth of the day and the cycle of renewal were gifts from the earth. It felt good to be alive. Thinking nothing at all, I fell into a light trance and the time passed quickly.

It was late afternoon, and the first rumble of thunder rolled out of the west.

We had come to the outskirts of Springfield.

Scattered near us were random groups of log cabins. Among them was the occasional log house, similar to those I had known in Salem. Like Sam Hill's house, some had a second story.

As we trotted further into the town, a mixture of log houses, wood frame structures, and occasional brick buildings lined the broad streets—a blend of homes and stores. Some of the stores offered dry goods, groceries, clothing, and shoes. Across the street were a tailor and even a barber. Down the next block was a hotel with a livery stable.

There we encountered several hogs, two cows, and a stray horse wandering toward us. None of their owners was in sight.

I became aware of a putrid stench. Looking down, I could see that it rose from piles of manure from these animals roaming the town at will. Garbage was randomly strewn into the streets.

The spring rains turned central Springfield's streets into rivers of mud. They sucked Pumpkin and me into the slop. She could barely move. Her legs were mired in over a foot of mud. A carriage with two horses and well-dressed passengers raced around the corner, and drenched us in black muck. Then our way was blocked by a group of hogs. Some of them were rooting up the wooden platforms that served as the town's sidewalks.

When I noticed a cabinetmaker's store, I decided to stop in and make my first purchase. I tied Pumpkin to the railing, entered the store, and contracted with the clerk for a bedstead. That done, I was back on Pumpkin and looking for a store that offered bedding.

Down two blocks was a large store with an inviting sign: JAS. BELL & CO: GENERAL MERCHANDISE. I decided that would be fine for my next purchases. Although it started to rain, Pumpkin was happy to be tied to the railing, under the overhang of the store's roof, and out of the deeper mud.

I climbed the stairs, opened the door, and walked into the general store. It was a large room with the merchandise organized into sections. In front were the dry goods, while behind them in the center and toward the far wall were shelves of groceries, medicines, books, and hardware. To the left side was clothing; mattresses and bedding were on the right.

There was a loud clap of thunder and the sound of rain pelting down on the roof.

Seated at a table near the center was a pleasant-faced young man who was poring over sheets of paper. As I came closer, I saw that on them were small rows of numbers.

He looked up and greeted me with an eager smile.

"May I be of help?" he asked.

In the deep of the night on my bench by the courthouse, I had gradually nodded off. The last image I remembered was the pleasant young man in the general store. My reverie ended, and I awoke to an odd sensation.

A warm, slimy object was pushing up my pant leg and exploring the skin of my left shin. I felt bristles rubbing against my skin and periodic puffs of warm air moving over it. Then came an even stranger feeling: a bulging, wet mass rasping over me.

Roused from my musings, I looked down to see a large hog, one of the very creatures about which I had been dreaming, licking my lower leg. I was sure it meant no harm, but I pushed it away. It grunted and snorted its way back into the muddy street.

Jarred back into the deep darkness, I rose slowly from the bench. Over my head, an owl whirred past causing a momentary rush of air. Landing on a hitching post, it inspected the ground below for mice. I froze, and we watched each other patiently before it flapped away toward the forest.

I walked across the mud-slopped street to Speed's store and climbed the steps to claim my half of the bed.

I lay down and slept soundly.

Chapter Three

I Would Take General Adams Down

Morning brought the day when the junior partner of the law firm of Stuart and Lincoln, 4 Hoffman Row, was to begin his law career in Springfield. Stuart was an early riser and expected me in the office at 7:30. I bade a good morning to Speed, dressed, and hurried downstairs. As I was not one for breakfast, I was out the door and onto the wooden sidewalks of the town square.

Hoffman Row was just a block north of Speed's store. When the bell from one of the churches tolled seven times, I decided to take a leisurely walk around the square. I started south on Fifth Street until I reached Adams. The early light, a pinkish glow, rose above the roofs of the buildings to the east.

The county courthouse presided over the center of the square. Two stories high, made of bricks with a cupola on top, it looked new. It was surrounded by a low cut of grass that was beginning to turn green. This was where I'd be spending much of my time in the months ahead. Strolling along Adams, I looked up at the courthouse.

I began to think about what I hoped to accomplish as a lawyer. Why had I chosen this work? When we'd served together in the legislature, Stuart encouraged me to read his law books. That was the first step. In addition, many of my colleagues were lawyers, and, if I wanted to continue in politics, a familiarity with the law was necessary. When I read Blackstone, I felt my mind embracing the logic that was central to an understanding of the law.

I believed that I could infuse a moral tone into my work. Lawyers were sometimes ridiculed as dishonest, but this shouldn't be true if the lawyer gained his client's confidence and trust. Above all, I would be honest, and I would strive for the honor a lawyer could achieve for himself through his work.

The way to Stuart's office took me north on Sixth Street to Washington. There I turned left and walked west. This was the section of the square with run-down stores known as "Chicken Row" for the poultry sold there. Looking ahead, I noticed how broad these streets were in the center of the town. There was room for several horse carriages to pass each other. As the streets rolled away from the square, trees stood watch over the wooden sidewalks. Coming to the corner of Washington and Fifth Street, I crossed over and strode north.

Several two-story brick buildings formed Hoffman's Row. When I climbed the stairs to the second floor of the fifth building, I saw the small, but newly painted sign for STUART & LINCOLN, Attorneys and Counsellors at Law. I stared at it. That couldn't be me. I traced my fingers over the letters in disbelief. The tingling in my fingers ran up my forearms, into my shoulders, and down my spine.

I rapped on the door.

When it opened, I was greeted by an elegantly dressed gentleman who was two years older than I.

Stuart grew up in Kentucky and had been to Centre College. Two years later, he was licensed to practice law, moved to Springfield, and began to take clients. When he came in 1828, it was a village of 300 people, and since then, he had become very well connected.

We had known each other in several different settings. We met during the Black Hawk War and grew close when we journeyed home together after our discharge from the militia. He ensured my election to the legislature by deflecting the Democratic opposition away from me and toward himself; the Democrats' strategy failed, and we were both elected. He had even roomed with me in a boardinghouse in Vandalia.

This was the gentleman who greeted me at the door that morning. He was very attractive with balanced features, a prominent forehead, and piercing eyes. Everything about his manner reflected self-assurance.

He led me into the office and offered me one of the two chairs at the simple table in the center of the room. The table was covered with piles of papers, opened books, and pens lying next to an inkwell.

"Good morning, Lincoln. I trust you have had a suitable welcome to Springfield," he began.

"Yes, Stuart, I am suitably introduced to the hogs, the mud, and the ungodly stench of our new state capital."

With a wry smile, he eyed me and said, "And soon to be joined by the dreadful smashing of sledgehammers demolishing our county courthouse—the result of your growing political skills."

"Which I learned from you," I added.

He laughed and relaxed back in his chair.

"I must say, Lincoln, I congratulate you and the others for convincing the legislature to give up Vandalia and move the capital here. As you've no doubt seen, Springfield is bursting at the seams."

"That would be true if there ever had been any seams," I said as I leaned toward him. "The growth seems willy-nilly at best."

"Yes, they seem to be working from the center out. The plan for the capitol building has been approved, hence the removal of our relatively new courthouse. Your friend, Dr. Henry, has been appointed the commissioner to supervise the construction."

Dr. Henry was indeed my friend. He'd come to Springfield in 1832, started a medical practice, and become a Whig politician. In 1836, after my duties as postmaster in New Salem ended, I kept a surplus of $16. When a government official came to collect, Dr. Henry offered to pay it for me. There was no need. I did not spend money that was not mine.

"It looks like Dr. Henry could help with this office," I said casting my eyes toward a place in the ceiling where the plaster had fallen. "It's like the capitol in Vandalia when we were first in the legislature."

"Oh, come now," he parried, "Hoffman Row is a step up from many other buildings in Springfield." He pointed to the water stains on the walls. "They are working on those, and have offered to repair the ceiling."

"And the courtroom downstairs is an advantage as well," he continued. "If you want to know what's going on, all you have to do is lower that trap door in the corner."

The office was sparsely furnished. Aside from the table and two chairs, against one wall there was a high, glassed bookshelf with a small built-in desktop. Between three tall windows at the far end, a bookshelf was crammed into the limited space. Another bookshelf and a small bedstead rested next to the other wall, while Stuart's buffalo robe hung from a hook midway between them. There were also two simple chairs that could be drawn up to the table if necessary. The drab bindings of the law books offered little color to the bland surroundings.

I had been in the office before, but on this day, it seemed different. I couldn't wait to get started. He seemed to sense what I was thinking.

"Well, Lincoln, shall we begin?"

I nodded.

"All right then, I'll ask you to draft the documents for the cases I have here on the table. That should take the better part of this week. Most of them are for the collection of debts, but there's one here for assault. That should be moderately interesting.

"Your handwriting is neat and clear, if not attractive. Your spelling is better than most, although I'm surprised you spell prosecutor with a second s. Aforesaid is not A-f-f-o-r-e-s-a-i-d or a-f-o-r-s-a-i-d, and allege does not have a d in it. Just give it more careful attention.

"You'll be keeping our books. It's tedious and it does take time, but you'll learn to do it. We split all earnings—50% apiece. I'm told that I don't charge as much as I should. You can look into that. We seem to make it up with the large number of cases we handle.

"We'll ride the circuit together this fall. I don't care for it, but you may enjoy it. It's a roving band of lawyers and judges who supplement their incomes by hearing cases in backwater county seats—too itinerant for me. It goes on for two months. Most of us come and go as we please, and I go home on the weekends.

"I've decided to give you a few cases up at the McLean County Courthouse so you can learn on your own. There's this fellow, John W. Baddeley, who wants us to represent him. He's a merchant in McLean. Probably another debt collection case. Go up there and see what that's all about. He wasn't very forthcoming, so you'll have to find out more from him.

"There's also a case here that I want to go over with you. If we handle it together, you'll be doing all this by yourself before long.

"Just one more thing: you know that I ran for Congress against William May last year and lost. I'm hearing that he won't run again, and that Stephen Douglas will be the Democrats' choice to keep the seat. I'm eager to take him on. He's a smart, scrappy little man, but I'd like to beat him. I'll be gone when that gets started, so we need to get you ready as soon as we can."

"What is the case that we'll be working on together?"

He sifted through the pile of papers and, after a few unsuccessful attempts, found several pages enclosed together by a sheet folded in half. It was spotted with coffee stains.

"Ah, here it is," he declared, "Cannan versus Kenney for Illegal Possession of Property."

"It seems that last fall, this fellow, Manly Cannan, was at work in the lead mines up near Galena. I expect he was an immigrant—English or Irish—who came here within the last five years. A friend of his, John Harris, was also working in the mines. Harris wanted to return home here in Sangamon County. Cannan loaned him his horse, which he expected Harris to return. When Cannan came back to Sangamon County, he found that one, Matthew Kenney, was in possession of the horse with no intention of giving it back.

"Cannan has retained us to sue Kenney for illegal possession of property. That's the formal declaration for what Cannan wants—to get his horse back. It seems sensible enough to me."

"Is there a description of the horse?" I asked.

"Yes, there is. Somewhere in here," he said, reaching for the clump of papers.

Stuart shuffled through them and pulled out a tattered envelope.

He read from the back of it, "Light sorrel horse—ball face—white feet—fifteen hands high—five years old—taken in March 1837. Witnesses: John Harris, John Anderson, and Joseph Smith."

"Does the horse have a value?"

"Indeed it does. Quite valuable in fact. Value is set at one hundred dollars."

"What will we seek for damages?"

"Two hundred dollars."

"Will we file in the action of trespass?"

"Indeed we will. You will write the declaration and it should state '...with force and arms, seized, took, and carried away of him the said Cannan one sorrel horse of great value, towit of the value of one hundred dollars, then and there found and being, and converted and disposed of the same to his own use, and other wrongs to the said Cannan....'"

"A file of trespass vi et armis?" I asked.

"Yes, that's the way it's done. It may seem to overstate the case, but it's inclusive. The force may be actual or tacitly understood. We must show that even though Cannan was in Galena when Kenney gained possession of his horse down here, it is the same as if Kenney were up in Galena."

"When would you like me to complete the declaration?"

Before he could reply, we were disturbed by a knock on the door.

Stuart rose from his chair, walked over to the door, and opened it.

Standing tentatively in the doorway were a simply dressed country woman accompanied by a younger man.

The similarity of their facial features indicated he was, in all likelihood, her son.

"Good morning," said the courtly Stuart. "Welcome to the office of Stuart and Lincoln."

The woman greeted him by saying, "I recognize you, Mr. Stuart. You may not remember me, but I met you during your congressional campaign."

"Then won't you please come in and join us," replied Stuart. "Mr. Lincoln and I are delighted to be of service."

"Thank you, Mr. Stuart," she said. "I am Mary Anderson and this is my son Richard. We live just north of Springfield. We have a matter we would like to discuss with you and Mr. Lincoln."

We fetched the other chairs, and the Andersons joined us at the table. Stuart made a half-hearted attempt to straighten the scattered papers.

"What can we do for you this morning, Mrs. Anderson?" Stuart asked.

She began, "I appreciate this opportunity to speak with you and Mr. Lincoln. You may have heard that my husband Joseph died recently."

Stuart replied, "No, Mrs. Anderson, I did not know. Please accept condolences on behalf of Mr. Lincoln and myself."

"Thank you, Mr. Stuart. I appreciate your kindness. My husband was a fine man, and our loss is a deep one. Unfortunately, the matters of his estate have been forced upon Richard and me.

"My husband owned 10 acres of land near our property north of Springfield. There were two 5-acre parcels. After my husband's estate is settled, Richard and I plan to sell this land. No sooner had we notified the surveyors of our intent, when we learned that General James Adams occupies one of the parcels."

"This must be the same James Adams who is probate justice of the peace—the very man against whom Dr. Henry is running in the election this August," I interjected.

"Indeed," said Stuart, "It can't be any other."

"Yes," added Richard, "It's the very man."

Stuart asked, "Madam, how did this come to be?"

Mrs. Anderson spoke in a low, sad tone, "My poor husband was very trusting. I'm afraid General Adams took advantage of him. General Adams was Joseph's attorney, and he claims that Joseph gave him the parcel."

Stuart asked, "Does he have title to the land?"

"He claims to have it. I believe he has gained it by foul means. Is it possible that his deed is fraudulent?"

"It is possible," said Stuart.

"We have confronted General Adams. He has reasserted his claim, and he refuses to relinquish possession of the property," she added.

Richard came directly to the point, "We wish to retain your firm to sue General Adams and regain possession of our property."

Stuart spoke for us, "Mr. Lincoln and I will consult on this matter. If we agree to represent you, I will ask you to forward all documents in your possession that pertain to your ownership of the land. If you have any correspondence between your husband and General Adams, we will need that as well.

"It could be that Judge Logan might like to partner with us on this case. No one is more respected in Springfield. He would be a strong advocate for you."

"Thank you both for your interest and consideration," said Richard.

"We will let you know early next week. When we next meet, we will discuss an appropriate fee," said Stuart.

We both rose and bade them good fortune and farewell.

When they had left, Stuart welcomed me back to the table, and we eased into our chairs.

"What is your inclination?" he asked.

"Can you have any doubt?" I shot back.

"You have no doubts?"

"Adams has a terrible reputation. He has clearly stolen this land from an unsuspecting widow and her only son," I replied.

"Don't be hasty, Lincoln."

I was confounded.

"Adams is a man of dubious reputation," said Stuart. "He is a braggart and a buffoon. In Springfield's first murder trial in 1826, he defended Nathan Van Noy. Thanks to Adams, Van Noy was found guilty and hanged. Adams's claim of being a general is questionable. He may have been sympathetic to the British in 1812."

"So he is a scoundrel!" I protested.

"Yes, he is, but what if the husband made the offer to General Adams. Adams was his attorney. He may have paid Adams by offering him one of the lots."

"That can't be true."

"How do you know?"

"But, Stuart, do you not see? Not only do we recover the land, but we expose Adams and destroy his chances for reelection. Dr. Henry will be the new probate justice of the peace!"

"Aha, a double motive! The politics trumps the young lawyer's judgment," he chortled.

I started to challenge him, but thinking better of it, I kept silent.

He paused and then continued, "I am thinking that we will take the case on contingency. If we should recover the land for the Andersons, our fee will be half the second parcel which we will split with Logan. Are you comfortable with that?"

"I am."

"Then I suggest you go over to the office of the Recorder to dig up whatever you can find."

I spent the rest of the day drafting documents for our cases. I started with the declaration for Cannan versus Kenney. When I wasn't certain about a detail, I consulted with Stuart. By late afternoon, I had made steady progress on it.

When we finished for the day, I walked back around the square. This time I reversed the direction of my morning walk. On Washington, "Chicken Row" was on my left. I turned right on Sixth Street, walked south, and then west on Adams.

I was still vexed by the Andersons' grievances against General Adams. Stuart counseled caution, but I was certain he had swindled the Andersons out of their land. Not only that, but when he was asked to return it, he arrogantly denied any wrongdoing.

I could help my friend Dr. Henry, and we could win the case for the Andersons and recover their land.

I would take General Adams down.

Chapter Four

"WHO IS WRITING THIS?"

G eneral Adams struck first.
He wrote an anonymous letter attacking Dr.
Henry in the *Illinois Republican*, the Springfield newspaper representing the Democrats. He claimed that Dr.
Henry had been negligent in his duties as a commissioner for the building of the new state capitol. This set
off a dispute that caused chaos in Springfield.

Dr. Henry's friends, including Sheriff Garret Elkin,
attacked the office of the newspaper. The next day, after
they were charged with disorderly conduct, the sheriff
whipped George Weber, the editor of the *Republican*,
almost killing him. Weber's brother then stabbed Elkin
with an eight-inch knife.

To calm the town, Stuart offered to convene a bipar-
tisan investigation, which later cleared Dr. Henry of any
improper conduct.

On June 22, Stuart and I joined with the firm of Logan and Baker to file a lawsuit against General Adams
on behalf of the Andersons. I was confident we would
win back the land General Adams had stolen. We would
also help Dr. Henry win the election for probate justice
of the peace and humiliate General Adams in the bargain. It was a delicious prospect.

The gatherings in Speed's store had started spontaneously. That first evening, when Speed and I sat beside
the fireplace and began to share our experiences, was
the precursor of many conversations we would have
over the next two months. The spring weather was cool,
and we spent our evenings bathed in the warmth and
glow of a crackling fire.

One evening, we hit on an idea together. "Let's invite
the others!"

Thence began the nightly gatherings by the fireplace in Speed's store.

The regulars were Stephen Douglas, John Hardin, Edward Baker, and Speed and I.

All of us except Speed were aspiring politicians. We were intensely ambitious, and we knew ambition could tear us apart. Even though Hardin, Baker, and I were all Whigs, we were rivals for position in the party. Douglas was a Democrat and therefore a political opponent. His ambition was like a steamboat; it would run over anything in its way. Nevertheless, we all liked him. What held us together for the moment was our fierce desire to promote the interests of Springfield and the state of Illinois.

Politics, religion, philosophy, poetry—we discussed them all. There were evenings of literary recitations—passages any of us knew by heart, original poems and other literary productions, and an occasional scene from a play by Shakespeare.

We engaged in verbal jousting: quips and barbs were fair play. Jokes, sometimes droll, and stories, not always appropriate, were told with entertaining and ironic flourishes.

In late July, the regulars gathered for another evening in Speed's store. With the stifling summer heat, we had no fire, but from the stones of the hearth and the fireplace, we could feel occasional wisps of cooler air.

At the beginning of the evening, Speed did something very unusual. He stood in front of the fireplace and raised his voice to make an announcement.

"I have some news," he shouted.

At first we ignored him, but, as he seemed more intent than usual, gradually we stopped talking.

"I have some news," he repeated, "Isaac Melton has asked a favor of us."

"Who is Isaac Melton?" asked Hardin.

"We know each other quite well," replied Speed. "He's vice president of the Springfield Mechanics Union. He's in here all the time."

"What can he possibly want from us?" inquired Baker.

"He's making up the program for their fall Harvest Festival, and he came in here this morning with an idea. He asked if our local politicians would be willing to do a short theatrical. When I asked what he had in mind, he said last year some of the Union members had seen a theater company perform *A Midsummer Night's Dream*. They thought the scenes with the workers were very funny. He suggested you could perform one of those scenes."

"A capital idea!" yelled Douglas, "I shall play Bottom."

Speed ignored him and continued, "Melton says if we perform the casting scene first, perhaps we could do the rehearsal in the woods next year, and the play itself the following year."

"I have no idea what's going on," said Hardin.

"Let him continue," interjected Baker.

"But I don't remember anything about this play."

"Hardin, don't be such an ass. You don't have to know anything about it," scowled Baker.

"Next year I get to play the ass," chuckled Douglas.

"No one is playing anything until I finish," cried Speed. "Will someone please explain the play to Hardin?"

Before anyone else could speak, Douglas chimed in, "I'll do it! Hardin, it's really very simple. The workers have been asked to perform a play for a king who is celebrating his wedding. They choose the tale of Pyramus and Thisby, two lovers who run away and meet near a wall by moonlight. Since I am Bottom, I get to play Pyramus. Thisby is eaten by a lion, and Pyramus kills himself."

Hardin looked very mystified and asked, "Why would they do something like that for the king?"

Baker explained, "Well, they're simple people and they don't know any better."

I had enjoyed being in the audience, but it was time for me to speak up.

"Speed, we should do this. We can't refuse their invitation. You should play the part of Peter Quince and cast us for the scene."

The others agreed, and Speed looked pleased as he continued with his plan.

"All right, then, I shall play Peter Quince, and here are your roles. Douglas, you will be Bottom."

When he heard this, Douglas cavorted around the room, skipping and dancing and crowing with glee.

"What is my part?" asked Baker.

"I have given this considerable thought. Baker, you shall have a part with no words."

Baker scrunched his face and said, "I will not play a woman."

"Oh, good heavens," said Hardin, "There's a woman in this scene? One of us will have to play a woman?"

"Indeed, and remember in Shakespeare's time, the women's parts were played by men. Baker, your part is not Thisby."

"If no one else will play Thisby, I shall play Thisby," interrupted Douglas.

"Douglas, you cannot be both Pyramus and Thisby. Baker, your part will be the lion. It is nothing but roaring."

Baker jumped up and began to roar at everyone, saving a last, enormous roar for Douglas. When he had roared himself out, he sat down and asked, "Who will play the woman?"

"I have given that considerable thought as well. Lincoln's role will be Francis Flute who plays Thisby."

"Well done, Speed," cried Baker, "Lincoln is perfect as the woman. His voice is high pitched, unlike those of us who have mellifluous baritones."

"Perhaps by playing a woman, I will understand them better than any of you," I responded.

"And what is my part?" asked Hardin.

"You have a very difficult one, for you have two parts."

"But you said no one can have two parts."

Douglas smirked.

"Your parts have no words, and, essentially, they are one and the same. You shall play both the wall and the moon. You will have a lantern by which you will light yourself."

"Speed, well done once more," yelled Baker, "for Hardin is a man of few words , no imagination, and stiff as a board. He will make an admirable wall!"

"Well, gentlemen, as Peter Quince doth say, 'Here is a play fitted.'"

The next afternoon, after work, I took a long walk through the town. This was a pleasure I began to give myself each day. I was starting to feel more comfortable in Springfield.

Although some of my work as a lawyer was menial, the principles of the law spoke to me. I tried to encourage my clients to settle their differences. I discouraged litigation. There were lawyers who fed on litigation, but the winner was often a loser from fees, expenses, and wasted time. I wanted to be a peacemaker. These goals were guiding me in my daily work.

I was fortunate to have Stuart as a mentor. Though I would never adopt his refined manner or equal his social grace, some of his polish was rubbing off on me, particularly in the courtroom. Because he was getting ready to run again for a seat in Congress, he gave me some of our important cases. At first, I felt unprepared, but with experience I was gaining confidence.

My friendships, which had been based on political views and practice, were becoming personal. We shared our triumphs and failures, and could laugh at and with each other.

In late July, we met again for another evening in Speed's store. Several of us had just come back from the special session of the legislature in Vandalia which concluded on July 22.

The issue that consumed us was the same one that had divided the legislature: how to respond to the economic panic that gripped the country that spring. In the previous legislative session, we passed $10,000,000 of internal improvements for Illinois to be funded by state bonds. With the country in financial collapse, Governor Duncan called for repeal of the internal improvements legislation. The legislature opposed him and pushed full speed ahead with the plans to provide for the construction of canals and railroads in Illinois. With the exception of Baker, we Whigs led the charge.

In the informal setting of Speed's store, we were debating these issues again.

Baker stepped forward and spoke first, "It all goes back to Andrew Jackson. With his horror of debt, his hatred of the elite, and his posturing for farmers and laborers, he destroyed the Bank. He—"

"Baker, not this again," Douglas interrupted, "haven't we done with it? Jackson vetoed the re-charter of the Bank because it was a threat to the sovereignty of the American people. You Whigs need to accept once and for all that America is a democracy."

With a flourish, Baker turned on Douglas. "Nonsense, Douglas, we Whigs support the common man more than you do. You deceive him. You Democrats oppose the market economy. We want a financial system that works for rich and poor. The country needs a stable currency to support it. The Bank provided that. Jackson disapproved of paper money and was a fool to tear down the Bank. He is responsible for the depression."

We had been over this so often that I tried to take it in a different direction.

"The question now is what happens to the Illinois state bank," I counseled.

"And much good you have done for that," countered Baker. "I was opposed to your reckless scheme for running up so much debt to pay for all the construction. You have put the state on the road to financial ruin."

"No, my friend, I think not. Every dollar we spend on improvements for our state will yield a handsome return. It will just take time."

"Tell that to the investors who will get 40 cents on the dollar. I'm with Governor Duncan. We should have repealed the bill."

Hardin was reading the *Sangamo Journal*, and growled from behind his newspaper. "The Journal has finally published the speech Daniel Webster gave when he was here in June. Listen to this:

'Is there an intelligent man in the community, at this moment who believes that, if the Bank of the United States had been continued, if the deposits had not been removed, if the specie circular had not been issued, the financial affairs of the country would have been in as bad a state as they are now?'"

Douglas went into retreat, and tried to save face by firing a salvo at me. He changed his focus to the recent two-week special session of the legislature.

"Lincoln," he roared, "Weren't you chosen by the Whigs to speak against Ewing's bill to reestablish Vandalia as the state capital?"

"I was," I asserted.

"Hah," he chortled, "and I hear he declared, 'Gentlemen, have you no other champion than this coarse and vulgar fellow to bring into the lists against me? Do you suppose that I will condescend to break a lance with your low and obscure colleague?'"

Before I could reply, Hardin interrupted with urgency in his voice. "Gentlemen, there's another of those Sampson's ghost letters in the *Journal*!"

Baker asked, "What's that?"

"You haven't heard?" Hardin replied, "Someone's been attacking General Adams in the *Journal* with letters from Sampson's ghost."

"What's that?" Baker repeated.

"Well, General Adams claims he owns land north of town, but he's contested by the Andersons whom

Lincoln is representing. There's been a series of letters from this Sampson's ghost who purports to be the spirit of one Sampson who was the previous owner."

"I thought the Andersons were the previous owners," interjected Speed.

"No," said Hardin, "Adams says they have no claim to the land at all. Listen to what this ghost says, 'and I again call upon the General to explain to the citizens of this county by what authority he holds possession of the ground in Springfield upon which he now resides.'"

"Who is writing this?" asked Douglas, "Usually it's not hard to tell. I find it amusing, but I'm sure the General doesn't."

"Probably someone who has a motive for attacking him," observed Baker.

Hardin started to laugh.

Baker seemed confused, looked sternly at Hardin and asked, "You find this amusing?"

"No, no," responded Hardin, "There's something else in here about General Adams. It seems to be a story from another anonymous source."

He continued reading, "The recent noise and excitement made about the wounds and bruises received by Gen. Adams, reminds me of an adventure which happened to me while traveling to this county many years ago. Not far from this place I met a sucker late in the evening returning to his home. 'Good evening friend,' said I. 'How far is it to Springfield?' 'Well, I guess it's about five miles.' 'Are you just from there?' 'Well, I am,' and said I, 'What's the news there?' 'Well, there's nothing of any account but a sad accident that happened the other day—you don't know Gineral Adams?—Well, the Gineral went to stoop down to pick some blackberries, and John Taylor's calf gave him a butt right—'You don't say so—and did the Gineral die?' 'No, by G..., but the calf did!'"

The assembled collapsed in guffaws and fits of laughter. When Hardin subsided, Douglas chortled once more—and that started it all over again.

When the laughter finally ceased, Hardin asked emphatically, "Who is writing all this?"

I strode toward the fireplace, stood in the center of the hearth, faced them, and cried, "Gentlemen, I am the one!"

With the exception of Baker, they seemed genuinely shocked.

When Speed recovered, his eyes flashed at me as he said, "Lincoln, you will try him both in court and in the newspapers? That is not right."

"Speed, we must win the land back for the Andersons and the election for Dr. Henry. All I wish is truth shall prevail."

"But Lincoln, in those letters, you haven't told the truth yourself."

"No, Speed, you just don't know how the game is played."

"Well, if nothing else," shouted Douglas, "I find this damned amusing. Lincoln, you have gotten yourself into a pickle."

"No, Douglas, you are the one most often pickled."

"Pickled be damned," he retorted, "you prattling teetotaler. General Adams will dispose of you with relish."

"Not so," I cried, "I will publish a handbill two days before the election claiming that General Adams forged the deed by which he claims to hold title to the land!"

Baker stood up and confronted me, bristling with anger, "Two days before an election? How can you do that? It's shameful, Lincoln. You give him no time to reply."

Hardin joined in on Baker's side, "Lincoln, those letters you've been writing are contemptible. You have no evidence. It is foul play. Your handbill will turn people against Dr. Henry, and he will lose the election."

"You are wrong," I bellowed at them like a wounded boar, but I could not convince them of the merits of my case.

I did circulate my anonymous handbill just before the election. In it, I gave the evidence for the charge that General Adams had forged the deed to the Anderson property.

Two days later, General Adams defeated Dr. Henry for the office of probate justice of the peace. There were 1,025 votes for General Adams and 792 for Dr. Henry. The Illinois Register claimed that General Adams had won by such a large margin because the voters were angered by the smear campaign conducted by the *Sangamo Journal*. My friends were right; my plan had backfired.

The lawsuit we filed against the General was mired in procedural issues. We had made no progress in wresting the land from Adams and returning it to the Andersons.

Chapter Five

WHAT I WRESTLE WITH EACH DAY

In late October, a fashionably dressed gentleman knocked on the door of the office of Stuart and Lincoln. Stuart and I ushered him in to have a seat at our untidy table. I drew up a chair for him, and the three of us took our places.

"Gentlemen, I have a tale of woe," he began. "Perhaps you have heard of me. I am Joseph Jefferson, the proprietor of a theater company from New York. My father founded our company, I am the present owner, and my son will succeed me. We were all born on the boards, and it is in our blood."

"I have heard of you, Mr. Jefferson," I replied. "In a manner of speaking, I understand your ship has crashed on the rocks of the Springfield town council."

"Indeed, you are correct," volunteered Mr. Jefferson. "Young man, I did not catch your name."

"Abraham Lincoln, sir."

"Ah, now I understand. It was to Mr. Stuart that I was recommended."

"We are both at your service," said Stuart.

"Well, I am much cheered by that news," he said with a flourish. "You know then that my players, the Illinois Theatrical Company, were invited to perform in Springfield. Since we were asked to perform for the season, we decided to build a theater here—not a glamorous one by any means, but a functional one nevertheless. It is essentially a very small box, but it will do. No sooner was construction finished than the town council passed an unreasonable licensing fee on our 'unholy' profession. It is prohibitive, and we will not be able to perform."

"No doubt," said Stuart, "you are the casualty of our latest religious revival."

"I'm afraid so," replied Mr. Jefferson. "Will you represent our company if we appeal the decision of the city fathers?"

"What say you, Lincoln?" Stuart asked.

Here was the chance to take a very interesting case. My love of Shakespeare had grown into an appreciation of the theater. I could promote it in Springfield.

"We'd be delighted," I replied, "I will take the case without a fee."

The town council of Springfield scheduled my appearance for the following week. Because we were busy with so many other cases, I did not have much time to prepare.

On one of our evenings by the fireplace, before the others arrived, I asked Speed, "Will you listen to the close of my speech to the council?"

"By all means," he replied.

"Gentlemen," I contended, "the issue that has been before us this evening is significant because it will determine who we are as a community. Will we affirm our common humanity, or will we deny it? Will we extend our basic liberties to all, in this case, artists who seek only to entertain and enlighten us? It was Hamlet who said 'the purpose of playing… is to hold, as 'twere, the mirror up to nature….' Is this what you will not permit?

"Inscribed in the Temple of Apollo at Delphi is the phrase 'Know Thyself.' This is the great principle of self-knowledge which is rooted in the tragedies of Aeschylus, Sophocles, and Euripides. Thousands of citizens attended those performances in ancient Greece. It was a community ritual. The people of Elizabethan England and Shakespeare were their worthy successors. The Joseph Jefferson Company will stage a production of Macbeth. Surely you will not deny the citizens of Springfield the opportunity to be part of this great tradition. Please repeal the licensing fee that you have imposed on these players and let them perform."

"What do you think?" I asked him.

"Lincoln, if the rest of it is as good as that, you and I will be going to see Macbeth!" he replied.

Speed was right. I spoke to the town council at length, imploring them and occasionally joshing them. At the end of my presentation, they agreed to move the issue to a vote and rescinded the licensing fee. The Joseph Jefferson Theatre Company was back on the boards.

When I dropped in on Mr. Jefferson the next day, he was delighted with the result. He regaled me with stories of his company's trip from New York to Chicago and then eventually to Springfield. Traveling from Galena to Dubuque, they rode over the frozen Mississippi River in horse-drawn sleighs. There had been a few days of warm weather, and the ice was cracking and groaning. Unfortunately, the sleigh with the scenery, costumes, and props crashed through the ice. With luck, they came to rest on a sandbar from which they were rescued, but the performances were delayed a week.

At our parting, Mr. Jefferson rose and said, "Please, please, you must favor us with your presence at one of our performances of Macbeth."

"Thank you so much, Mr. Jefferson. I am honored. May I bring my good friend, Joshua Speed?"

"Of course, of course, we should be pleased to see Mr. Speed as well," he replied, sweeping the air with his hands and performing a mock bow.

A week later, Speed and I were walking the wooden sidewalks trying to keep our boots out of the mud which once again abounded in the streets of Springfield. We'd had late fall rains. Several dogs were tearing open the carcass of a hog which lay littering the street. We were on our way to the theater where Mr. Jefferson's company was performing Macbeth.

It was from Jack Kelso in New Salem that I first learned about Shakespeare's plays. There were excerpts in the readers I studied as a boy in Indiana, but when Jack recited passage after passage from the tragedies, I was entranced. He loaned me his copy of the plays, and I read them all. One of my favorites was Macbeth. I had never seen any of the plays performed, so Mr. Jefferson's invitation was full payment for the service I had rendered him.

We had a long walk because the theater was located in the outskirts of the town. Although it was small, from the distance, we could see the freshly cut wood of the building's exterior. It was crudely built, erected quickly for temporary use by the players.

Mr. Jefferson himself greeted us at the door. He led us into a building that he had correctly described as a small box. There was a stage at the front, and the audience sat on simple wooden chairs. Wooden blocks around the room served as sconces for whale oil candles. We presumed they would be snuffed out before the performance.

The lights on the stage appeared to be in some kind of a contraption. Speed asked Mr. Jefferson, "What is that?"

"Oh," he replied, "it works remarkably well. It's for the footlights. The lamps are set in a 'float' with counterweights. When the stage needs to be dark or the lamps need trimming, the mechanical contrivance sinks under the stage."

"I hope it doesn't set the theater on fire," said Speed earnestly.

"Oh, no," chortled Mr. Jefferson, "no worries about that, Mr. Speed, unless, of course, we should wish to reenact the sack of Troy!"

"You know," he continued, "for a theater in the West, this little one is quite advanced. You must understand that neither my partner, Mr. McKenzie, nor I have ever owned anything with a roof until now."

The patrons had taken their seats, and the theater was full. Mr. Jefferson led us to three seats he had reserved in the front row. He gave a brief welcoming speech and sat down to hearty applause. With the agility of a panther, a stagehand extinguished the candles in the house, and we were ready to begin.

The play was performed without an intermission. It took hold of me and never let go. I had never had an experience like it. The story of the play was frightful and frightening. I was riveted by Macbeth's descent into evil and Lady Macbeth's unraveling. The darkness of the theater had absorbed the darkness of the play. Did I have a connection with the man Macbeth and the monster he became? Did part of me understand Lady Macbeth's drive and how it undid her? Why did Macbeth come to trust the witches when Banquo didn't?

These were all questions I had as Speed and I leaped to our feet to applaud the players at the end.

When Mr. Jefferson turned to me, I could not speak.

"I know," he said. "That is the magic and the mystery. It transports us from ourselves and into another realm. If it's done as well as this, we return, ever so slightly, altered and renewed. Of course, that's the genius of Shakespeare!"

I looked into his eyes, gave him a nod, shook his hand firmly, and turned to Speed. He had been as affected as I. He shook Mr. Jefferson's hand, gave him a few words of thanks, and we left.

We hardly spoke on our walk back to the store. It was not awkward, as each of us was deep into his own thoughts. When we arrived home, after Speed poked the fire back into life, and warmth returned to the hearth, we collapsed into the comfortable wooden chairs nearby.

We gazed into the fire without feeling the need to converse.

Finally Speed broke the silence.

"There is a question I just can't seem to answer."

"And what is that?"

"Why does Macbeth kill the king?"

"Why do you find it so hard to understand?" I asked him.

"Because the Macbeth we meet in the first part of the play could not have done it."

"Why not?"

"He says he can't do it because he is the king's kinsman and his subject, and when Duncan is visiting his castle, he is his host."

"Anything else?" I asked, looking at him carefully.

"Yes, after he meets the witches, he says to himself, 'If chance will have me king, why chance may crown me without my stir.'"

He looked back into the fire, and then added, "After Lady Macbeth first admonishes him to kill the king, he tells her, 'We will proceed no further in this business.'"

"And then?"

"Lady Macbeth says she knows he wants to be king, she tells him he should act on that desire, and, if he doesn't, he's a coward."

"That is true, but is it enough to change his mind?"

"No, the witches are part of it."

"Yes, but is there anything else?"

"That's what I don't know."

We paused for a moment as he put another log on the fire and stirred it slowly. I stretched back in my chair and watched the flames rise to wrap themselves around Speed's latest offering.

I spoke deliberately, "It's three things: the witches' prophecies, his wife's urging, and his own ambition."

"But the third part is the one I don't see." He seemed puzzled, and added, "Lady Macbeth says he is filled with 'the milk of human kindness'; that what he wants 'highly,' he wants 'holily'; and that, although he has ambition, he doesn't have the driving desire to fulfill it. That's who Macbeth is to me at the beginning of the play."

"So you don't think he has ruthless ambition at the beginning?"

"No, I don't."

"What is Macbeth like once he has killed the king?

"He's a monster. He has no conscience. He kills Banquo and Lady McDuff and her little ones."

"And is he the same person he was at the beginning?"

"Heavens no!"

"Speed," I said, "that's where you go wrong, and why you don't understand him."

"How do you know?" he asked.

I looked toward the fire and said, "Because it is true for me as well."

"What are you saying?" he uttered in disbelief. "How can that be?"

"The seeds of Macbeth the monster are in him at the beginning of the play. It just takes the right set of events for them to sprout. The entire play is about how things appear on the surface and how they are underneath. Lady Macbeth advises him, 'Look like the innocent flower, but be the serpent under it.'"

"How can you see yourself as Macbeth?"

"I fear I may well be."

"I've lived with you for several months. I know you. Your ambition is strong, but it is balanced. It is our friend Douglas who is a prisoner to his ambition. His north star is his lust for power. That's not you."

"How do you know how ambitious I am?

"I can tell."

"But you are just looking at the surface. You don't know what lurks below."

"What can that possibly be?"

"What if my ambition knows no rest?"

"No one can answer that but you."

"Speed, I am afraid it is very dark."

"Are you asking if you can have deep ambition and still remain good?"

"Yes."

"Then you must wrestle with it."

"I do each day."

Personal ambition was gnawing at me, but at the same time, I was trying to focus on the greater good. Sometimes my ambition was a lone wolf tracking a wounded deer; it smelled the kill and could taste the bloody flesh. At other times, it was an eagle soaring over the prairie, watchful and ready—a cold, calculating, balanced force.

What was the proper role of ambition in my life? I was still searching for it.

Chapter Six

THE PERPETUATION OF OUR POLITICAL INSTITUTIONS

In the summer and fall of 1837, I began my law career in earnest. Because the cases in Springfield weren't enough for two lawyers, in the fall, Stuart traveled around the towns of the First Judicial Circuit, the 10 counties adjacent to Springfield. We called this "riding the circuit" because the lawyers rode on horses or in buggies. As soon as I felt comfortable in the courtroom, it would be my turn to ride the circuit.

Stuart was also distracted because he was planning for his upcoming race for Congress against Stephen Douglas. We expected a hard-fought campaign with the result in doubt until election day. Stuart would be devoting most of his time to the congressional race after the first of the year.

Although I wasn't ready for the circuit, Stuart sent me to Taylorville, a town to the southeast of Springfield, to argue a case for collecting a debt. The courthouse, sitting on stone pilings, was set above the ground. Unfortunately, this offered the town's hog population a perfect space to gather. During the trial, I was constantly interrupted by squeals and grunts from the coterie of hogs beneath the floor. It became so annoying that I halted my summation and asked the judge for a "writ of quietus" for immediate enforcement by the sheriff.

Another case that Stuart gave me was *Hawthorn v. Wooldridge*. Our client, Wooldridge, was sued by Hawthorn for not allowing him access to a cornfield for the use of which Hawthorn had already paid Wooldridge. When Hawthorn attempted to plough the land, the suit alleged that Wooldridge "struck, beat, bruised, and knocked him down; plucked, pulled, and tore out large quantities of hair from his head; with a stick and his fists he struck him a great many violent blows... violently hit, kicked , struck, and beat him... and with great violence, forced, pushed, thrust, and gouged his fingers into his eyes."

Hawthorn brought three suits against Wooldridge: breach of contract with demand for $100; *trespass vi et armis* with demand for $500 in damages; and a replevin suit for the return of "one black and white yoke of steers, one black cow and calf, and one prairie plow, with $20 in damages."

The details of the case were gruesome, but I decided to test my principle that, if possible, the opposing parties should come to a settlement. Hawthorn was represented by his attorneys, Walker and Hewitt. Here was another principle of the law. A lawsuit was the result of a conflict between two parties. Because the lawyers were more removed from the emotion of the conflict, they could approach the case more objectively.

In talking with Hawthorn's attorneys, we found the common ground on which we could negotiate. We were aided by the inevitable delays that occurred in legal action. The declarations for two of the suits were submitted in the summer of 1836 and the third in the fall. As time inched and then flowed away, the emotions began to heal, and the wound was not so raw. With time came the possibility of settlement and even reconciliation. One of the suits went to trial and the jury awarded Hawthorn $36 in damages and costs. With settlement of the two remaining suits, the plaintiff bore the costs of one, and the defendant the costs of the other.

Stuart was right. Some cases were more interesting than others. Many of our cases involved debt collection, trespassing, stolen livestock, business partnerships, wills, deeds, and contracts, with an occasional case of divorce or assault and battery. Our fees were mostly $5 or $10, which was enough to pay my room and board for a week or two. What I was learning was that drudgery was part of being a lawyer, but that care and precision were expected in the writing I did each day and the preparation I undertook for each case.

The evenings of political and literary discussions with our friends continued into the fall and early winter. Speed was an amiable host, and, as the nights grew colder, the crackling fires provided the warmth that drew us all together—that and the lively, and sometimes heated, discussions.

There were two newcomers to the group, both younger than most of us. Speed had hired Billy Herndon to clerk in the store, and he and Jim Matheny, who was the secretary of the Young Men's Lyceum of Springfield, frequently joined us.

A late November evening brought together Billy and Jim, Speed and me, and Edward Baker and Stephen Douglas.

Billy began with a report on the recent news that had shocked us.

"There's more now about how Lovejoy was murdered in Alton. Did you know that the mobs destroyed his printing press three times this year because of the abolitionist articles he'd been publishing in *The Alton Observer*?"

"Well, we heard about it the first time, but not much after that," said Baker.

Billy continued, "He ordered a fourth one. It had just come in, and he was storing it in a warehouse down by the river. The mob got wind of it, and that night, after they'd gotten liquored up, they surrounded the building. Lovejoy and his friends were inside and ready for them this time. The mob fired shots at them, and Lovejoy's men fired back. When the mob propped up a ladder to set the roof on fire, Lovejoy and a friend came out and knocked it over. When they tried a second time, Lovejoy came out again, and they shot him four times. He fell over and died. Then they destroyed the press and threw it in the river."

We were all silent for a little while.

Douglas spoke up, "The damned abolitionists and their radical notions are responsible for this violence."

"I wouldn't go that far," cautioned Baker.

"They are hated in both the North and the South. Lovejoy got what he deserved."

Baker continued, "Lincoln, you and Stone had something to say about this in the legislature, didn't you?"

"We did," I replied. "In March, we filed a statement after the passage of the resolution condemning abolition societies. We wrote, 'the institution of slavery is founded on both injustice and bad policy…'"

"Mush!" blurted Douglas.

"…but we also wrote, 'the promulgation of abolition doctrines tends rather to increase than to abate its evils.'"

"Well," interjected Speed, "Billy is also standing up for his principles."

"Yes," said Billy excitedly. "As you may know, I was a student at the college in Jacksonville. When the news of Lovejoy's murder first reached us, our teachers joined the students in protesting. My father heard about it and ordered me home. He's proslavery in his views. 'Billy,' he yelled, 'I am so angry about what you have done and what has happened at that college. I will no longer pay for you to attend. You will withdraw and come home.'"

"And the result is that I have a well-educated clerk to work for me at Jas. Bell & Co.," added Speed.

"And a well-paid one, too," burst out Billy. "Mr. Speed is paying me $700 a year!"

Speed smiled graciously.

"Drat, let's change the dreary subject of Lovejoy," said Douglas with a scowl. He then looked at me glee-fully and asked, "Lincoln, did you go up to McLean to represent some fellow called Baddelly?"

"I did."

"And what was the result?"

"I'd say it was unsatisfactory."

"Indeed, is that what you would call it?"

"Yes, I would."

"Friends," said Douglas slyly, "you have to hear about this. Our good friend Lincoln was sent by Stuart to see this fellow Baddelly, a rather gruff merchant up in McLean. It seems that Baddelly wanted Stuart to represent him on some legal matter. It takes Lincoln several hours to get there, and when he arrives, he calls on Baddelly. Baddelly takes one look at Lincoln and says, 'Just who are you?' Lincoln responds, 'I am hum-ble Abraham Lincoln sent here by my master, the noble John Todd Stuart, to represent you on your legal mat-ter.' 'Why,' says Baddelly, 'that cannot be. You are the most preposterous looking fellow I have ever seen in my life. You look like some yokel from Indiana. Your clothes do not fit, your face is ugly, and your hair is a mess.

That horse you have come on is a nag. How on earth can you pretend to be a lawyer? Please tell Stuart that I will have nothing to do with you. If he can't attend to this business himself, I will hire McDougall to represent me.' Whereupon he slammed the door, and Lincoln was left to trot back home on his nag!"

When he finished, he frowned triumphantly at me and asked, "Isn't this true, Lincoln?"

"Somewhat," I responded.

"Only somewhat?"

"Yes."

"Well, what's missing?"

"What's missing is the only thing he didn't call me was short."

The others all collapsed in laughter.

At this point, Jim Matheny spoke up. "This is just the time for us to switch from politics and the law to literature. I understand that Lincoln has written a poem on the frailty of women. To such poets as Shakespeare, Byron, and Pope, he now adds his widow's mite. There is but a fragment left for posterity."

Jim rose slowly and prepared to recite.

"An excerpt from 'Ode to the Frailty of Women' by Abraham Lincoln."

He looked at us, raised his arms and hands to frame his words, lowered his voice, and began:
"Whatever spiteful fools may say,
Each jealous, ranting yelper,
No woman ever went astray
Without a man to help her."

He sat down to laughter and applause and then said, "Now that this foolishness is over, we need to hear from Baker and Lincoln about the topics of their Lyceum addresses."

The Young Men's Lyceum was a group of men in Springfield who met from time to time to hear speeches about the issues of the day. Sometimes the speaker was a member of the Lyceum, and at other times he was from a different city. It was an honor to address the Lyceum, and I felt gratified that my invitation came within the first few months of my moving to Springfield. We met in the Baptist Church on the corner of Adams and Seventh Streets.

Baker had been invited to give his speech on January 13, 1838, and I was to address the Lyceum two weeks later.

Matheny prodded us, "Well, Baker?"

"You'll have to come hear it for yourselves," replied the cagey Baker.

"Lincoln?" Jim asked.

"The title of mine will be 'The Perpetuation of Our Political Institutions.'"

He followed up, "Could you clarify?"

"I'm concerned about the mob violence that is sweeping across our country," I said. "Our devotion to liberty will not survive if we cannot follow the rule of law."

"That's exactly what happened to Lovejoy," exclaimed Billy.

"I'll mention him," I said.

Douglas tried to dig deeper.

He probed, "Do you think our political institutions are in danger?"

"I do," I replied, "but you'll have to come to find out why."

On the evening of January 27, a freezing cold settled in over the prairie in mid-Illinois. The sky darkened early, and in the late afternoon, it started to snow. It did not deter the young men of Springfield from attending the event at the Young Men's Lyceum in the Baptist church. They wore their heavy coats and top hats as they walked the streets of Springfield. Once they reached the church, they were greeted by candles flickering throughout the nave. Although the candles could not provide heat on this frigid night, they did add cheer to the proceedings.

As the secretary of the Lyceum, Jim Matheny introduced me to the audience. He emphasized my achievements in the legislature, and he said I'd already earned my place at the bar in Springfield.

I stood at a lectern with the insignia of the Lyceum carved in front. I had spoken in court and the legislature, but this was different. This was my first formal address. The church was filled.

It was time for me to speak.

I began by reflecting on our republic in the year 1837.

The founders fought for and established a republic of liberty and equality to be governed by the people. Its political institutions took root and prospered.
The founders had died, and to us had fallen the task of preserving the republic.

I asserted that ours was a land of plenty with no danger of invasion. The two oceans on either side of our country prevented such a threat. From where then might danger come? If it were to arise, it would spring from among us. If destruction were to come, we ourselves would be its author.

Here I turned to the theme of my address: the increasing disregard for law in our country; the growing disposition to substitute the wild and furious passions of the mob for the sober judgment of the law and the courts.

A vicious portion of our population was gathering in bands of hundreds and thousands to impose its will by burning churches, throwing printing presses into rivers, shooting editors, and hanging and burning people at pleasure. The gamblers in Mississippi were hanged without a trial, and, in St. Louis, before he could be tried for murder, the mulatto man McIntosh was chained to a tree and burned. This was happening from New England to Louisiana. If it continued, our government would fall.

I then asked how we should strengthen ourselves against this danger. The answer was simple: that every American uphold the laws of the country, and never tolerate their violation by others. Reason must triumph over passion.

I then included a passage that reflected my deepest fear.

Men of talent and ambition would continue to emerge. For them, a seat in Congress, or a gubernatorial or presidential chair would suffice. But what if someone of towering genius arose, a man with sufficient ambition to push it to its utmost stretch—an Alexander, a Caesar, or a Napolean, a great tyrant like Macbeth—how would we resist his ambition?

It would require the people to be united with each other, attached to the government and laws, to frustrate his designs.

Inevitably, the living history of the revolution receded. The founders were the temple of liberty, but they crumbled away. Our task was to create new temples—not from passion—but from sober reason.

I concluded by saying that reason—cold, calculating, unimpassioned reason—must furnish all the materials for our future support and defense.

My Lyceum address was well received. The audience gave me warm applause. It was published in the *Sangamo Journal*. There was speculation about my reference to a towering genius with "vaulting ambition." Who could he be? The answer was that I did not know. What I did know was that someone with those gifts could emerge.

I had prepared carefully for the presentation, taking time late each afternoon to draft and revise the text. It had been a painstaking process, but through it, I learned that I could turn my thoughts into words and sentences that represented them accurately. The political principles in the Lyceum address had been gradually evolving in my mind. I was pleased with my ability to express them forcefully in a public address.

Giving the address to the Lyceum marked a turn for me. The opening scene of my time in Springfield ended. I felt more sure of myself as a lawyer. With Stuart's absence, I represented our partnership. The relationships with political associates and rivals deepened. Speed had become a kind and close friend. I was familiar with the streets of Springfield, and I loved to walk them, particularly at night. My confidence was deepening in my ability to grow, and I welcomed the challenges and rewards it brought.

PART TWO

Chapter Seven

THE POLITICAL EVENT OF THE YEAR

The congressional election of 1838 was the political event of the year. My friend, the Democrat Stephen A. Douglas, and my mentor, the Whig John Todd Stuart, were running for the seat in the third district. At the beginning of the campaign, Stuart and Douglas were friendly to each other. Although they were fierce political opponents, as long as they argued the issues, their relations were civil.

With election day on August 6, Stuart and Douglas began campaigning in January. For the next five months, they traveled together across the district. They rode in buggies or on horses in sunshine and in rain or snow. The roads were sometimes no more than horse paths or old Indian trails. They stayed at the same inns and taverns; stumped together at picnics, barbecues, and suppers; ate all their meals together; and slept in the same room.

In early June, I was in our office in Springfield reading through the documents from our latest cases. The table was strewn with papers, files, and letters—some were caked with mud from my boots. When Stuart was not in the office, I leaned back in my chair and propped my feet on the table.

Stuart had written he was on his way back to Springfield, and one morning, I heard the unmistakable sound of his footsteps ascending the staircase to our office. The door swung open, and Stuart, fashionably dressed as ever, entered the room. He gave me a broad, warm smile and shook my hand heartily. We sat down together at the untidy table.

"Lincoln," he said, "It is so good to see you!"

"Yes, Stuart, I've been expecting you ever since I received your letter."

"I'm delighted to be back in Springfield, if only for a brief visit. You must tell me about our cases, and doubtless you will want to know the latest about my contest with the Little Giant."

"I thank you for writing as often as you have," I replied. "Your instructions on the cases have been invaluable."

"From your questions, I see that you are picking up the finer points."

"With all the campaign events, how did you have time to write?"

He leaned back in his chair, put his hands on the back of his head with his elbows out to the side, looked at the ceiling, and sighed.

"I have always been an early riser. I attended to my correspondence before having breakfast with Douglas."

"Breakfast with Douglas?"

"Yes, he is a mess in the morning. He slurps his coffee, probably recovering from too much to drink and not enough sleep. I also have a story for you. You can add it to your repertoire of anecdotes."

"Is it about Douglas?"

"Yes, about our travels through the countryside.

"In Hancock County, we stopped over for the night in a small tavern. We retired early and were sleeping soundly when the innkeeper rapped on our door. It turned out that two guests were late arrivals because of the miserable weather. The innkeeper had given away their room, and there was no place to put them. Since there were four in all the other rooms, and since Douglas and I were the sole occupants of our room, the innkeeper's solution was to put them in with us. He suggested that we determine the sleeping arrangements.

"We were hardly presentable, but one of the late arrivals recognized Douglas. He inferred that I must be Mr. Stuart. 'Well,' said the other, 'my friend is a Whig, and I am a Democrat.' 'How propitious,' cried Douglas, 'Stuart, you take the Whig, and I'll take the Democrat.' With the sleeping arrangements concluded, we got into bed with our new friends and fell asleep once more."

"Well, it sounds as if you've done everything with Douglas short of making him your bedfellow."

"We are now two months from election day," said Stuart, "and I expect it to turn ugly. I understand you have been writing anonymous letters to the *Sangamo Journal* again. What pseudonym have you chosen this time?"

"Conservative."

"Have you gotten under his skin?"

"Indeed I have," I added.

I picked up my copy of the *Illinois Register* that was hiding under a nest of documents on the table.

"Listen to this whining from Douglas."

I then read from the *Register*. "Here is his response to one of my salvos: '…my private and moral, as well as public and political character has been assailed in a manner calculated to destroy my standing as a man and a citizen.'"

"Well done, Lincoln!"

"Isn't that the best way to treat so small a matter?" I asked.

"I wouldn't be quoted saying anything like that. You know how sensitive he is about being short."

"That may have been what set him off on Simeon Francis."

"What happened? I haven't heard."

This time it was my turn to tell a story.

"Douglas took offense to something Francis wrote in the *Journal*."

Stuart interrupted, "Francis is certainly within his rights unless it was libelous. After all, he is the editor."

"Well, it included a veiled reference to his size, and Douglas was enraged. He bought himself a cane and, intending to use it on Francis, walked over to the office of the *Journal*. There he found Francis who happened to be in the street. Douglas yelled at him. He then hit him in the back, the arms and legs, and over the head with his cane. Francis is taller than Douglas and just as fierce. He grabbed Douglas by his hair, which provided a proper handle, and dragged him over to a market cart in the street. There he propped the frightened little man against the cart and proceeded to pummel him. It took several men to pull Francis off Douglas. Everyone, except Douglas, found this quite amusing."

"I'm afraid," said Stuart, "it's a predictor of what's to come. Passions will run high in the last weeks of this race."

"I have written to Jesse Fell telling him, 'If we do our duty we shall succeed in the congressional election, but if we relax an iota, we shall be beaten.'"

"Right, Douglas is a formidable foe, but if we focus on the banks and the financial issues, we may have the advantage. The tide may be turning our way with the national economic disaster. The Democrats brought it on themselves by destroying the bank. I think our chances have improved for the next presidential election."

"We must press our advantage," I replied.

"Yes, and I hope you will continue to speak on my behalf. My lieutenants tell me you are forceful and engaging on the stump: humor and a touch of the slasher-gaff."

He paused and then continued, "But tell me, how are we progressing with some of our cases? Where are we on *Cannan v. Kenney*?"

I sorted through the files and found the one on the Cannan case.

"I prepared a bond for costs for Cannan in February, and he spent the next two months trying to find friends who would loan him the money. Unfortunately he was unsuccessful."

"He couldn't find anyone to make him a loan?"

"It appears not."

"That's not a good sign."

"It gets worse," I said.

"In March, the court ordered him to file a bond covering court costs. When he failed to do this, the court postponed the deadline until June 15. The case was continued to the next term. When Cannan finally did pay, the court found his bond wasn't for the full amount.

"I have met with Cannan, and he wants to dismiss the case. The court will accept this, provided he pays his and the defendant's fees. He will not be barred from filing suit against Kenney for the same offense in the future."

"And what about the Andersons' suit to recover their land from General Adams?"

"Continued to the next term as well."

"Ah, is it no surprise that we prefer the contest of an election to the uncertainty of the law?"

"But, Stuart, there is delay and uncertainly in politics as well," I replied.

"True, but the contest is decided on election day."

Stuart was right. The congressional race turned ugly in July and August. Not only was the campaigning heated, but as the summer progressed, it was one of the hottest and stickiest anyone could remember. We had day after day of torrid sunshine with no rain. The occasional thunderstorms provided no relief from the heat or the humidity. Everyone was on edge.

The newspapers led the charge.

The editorials in the *Illinois Register* attacked Stuart for being an upper-class dandy who had no interest in the farmers and the laborers who were the heart of the Democratic Party. As a Whig, he was charged with being an elitist who represented the wealthy and their interests. He was also lambasted for neglecting his law practice. Because of all his political maneuvering in the legislature, he was accused of being duplicitous.

The editorials in the *Sangamo Journal* countered that Douglas would be using the seat in Congress as a stepping-stone to higher office. He was portrayed as a young man in a hurry, someone who was not interested in his constituents. He was lampooned for being dwarfish. When Stuart was maligned for missing one of their debates, Douglas was pooh-poohed for being so small that he couldn't be seen at any of them. On top of all this came the charge that Douglas drank too much.

In early July, a month before election day, my Whig friends and I rode our horses to Jacksonville to hear Stuart and Douglas speak at a picnic. Jacksonville was the town to which Douglas had come when he first arrived in Illinois. The crowd was partial to him and roared, "Hit him again... skin him... lay it to him," when he hurled insults at Stuart. When Stuart taunted Douglas in his reply, the citizens yelled vulgarities back at him. The abuse continued throughout his long rejoinder to Douglas. In the late afternoon, Stuart's supporters retreated to a local tavern. Mugs of refreshing beer improved everyone's spirits.

We were relaxed and sharing stories from the campaign when Douglas and his cronies marched into the tavern. Both sides refrained from any interaction, until Douglas strode up to Stuart and challenged him about why he'd orchestrated such hurtful attacks. Stuart calmly said it all started with the editorials in the *Illinois Register*. Douglas shook his head and turned to rejoin his supporters.

Just then, someone on Stuart's side yelled out, "You ain't no Little Giant, you don't come up to Abe Lincoln's knees."

Douglas turned and rushed at Stuart. Stuart barely had time to defend himself, but he grabbed Douglas and began to tussle with him. Douglas pushed back, and the two of them careened around the room in each other's arms. Neither of them seemed to have an advantage, and they exerted Herculean efforts to little effect. They were deadlocked in a strange dance. Gradually Stuart began to push Douglas toward the floor, but Douglas fought back.

I was surprised they would brawl with each other, but each had been drinking liberally at the tavern. Douglas was unable to control his rage. Hardin was standing next to me, and he asked if we should intervene. Because it meant trying to separate two large, mad dogs, we refrained.

One of their wobbly gyrations brought them closer to a door near the kitchen. As they circled it, with a mighty lurch, Stuart pushed Douglas into the door. It exploded open and both combatants fell to the floor.

They writhed together in piles of slops. Little did they know that the entrance was the door to the butchery and on the floor were gobs of pig intestines.

Neither could wrestle the other into submission. First Stuart was on top, and then Douglas. Both were covered with the slime and blood from the discarded guts. Finally they fought themselves into exhaustion and then collapsed. Emotionally and physically spent, they helped each other up and limped back to rejoin their friends.

After the rivals cleaned themselves, Stuart and Douglas shook hands. Stuart asked to see the tavern keeper, and shortly thereafter it was announced that Mr. Stuart had bought a barrel of whiskey and a barrel of beer for the enjoyment of everyone present.

For a week or two after this incident, the tension in the campaign eased off a bit. Surrogates spoke for the candidates in debates across the district. There was no movement in our major cases, so I was tapped to speak for Stuart. Usher Linder, a political opponent with whom I was friendly, stood in for Douglas.We restricted ourselves to the issues.

As a Whig, I argued we were the party of those who wanted to rise and improve. We believed in a national bank to regulate our currency in support of a market economy. We favored government funding of internal improvements and a protective tariff to preserve jobs and protect industry.

Linder advocated for the Democrats as the party of the common man. He said they opposed a national bank because it concentrated wealth in the hands of a few. Arguing for a limited federal government, he believed that internal improvements should be financed privately. For the same reason, and because it would hurt the price of cotton, he opposed the tariff.

The crowds were interested in these discussions and refrained from goading us into insulting each other.

The truce ended in the first week of August, just three days before the election. The last debate featuring Stuart and Douglas took place in front of the Market House at Sixth and Washington Streets in Springfield. The summer heat and humidity were unbearable. Speed and I were in the huge crowd. The mood was uneasy. The long campaign had frayed the tempers of the candidates and their supporters.

When Stuart and Douglas took their places, partisans from each side roared and hooted at each other. Many in the crowd had spent the morning at their favorite tavern. The mayor tried to gain control over the proceedings.

He introduced Douglas who spoke first. Douglas had spent the morning with his allies at The Cock and Crown. He unloosed whatever restraint he felt after the embarrassing melee with Stuart in Jacksonville. If the insults in the *Illinois Register* had galled Stuart, they were nothing compared to the smears and slander, punctuated with curses and vulgarities, that Douglas hurled at him in front of the Market House.

With the reserve and presence of a gentleman, Stuart tried to ignore Douglas's barrage, but when Douglas assailed his character, he could bear it no longer.

On this occasion, Stuart attacked. He leaped from his chair, rushed at Douglas, and grabbed him by the neck. He hoisted a frantic Douglas into the air and carried him through the crowd which parted to make room for the spectacle. The Stuart partisans roared their approval.

Douglas, however, was not without defense. He leaned toward Stuart and gave him a horrid bite on his thumb. Stuart screamed, slammed Douglas onto the ground, and writhed in pain. The flesh on his thumb was torn open and bled profusely. A doctor in the crowd rushed forward to help bandage it. Douglas was still floundering on the trodden grass. Their last joint appearance of the campaign came to an end.

This time Stuart was at fault. But could he be expected to restrain himself from Douglas's ferocious attacks? It troubled me, and I had no answer. What would I have done? I did not know.

Stuart had one last speech scheduled for Bloomington. His hand developed a nasty infection, and he was weakened by a high fever. He asked me to represent him in Bloomington, and I obliged him with my last campaign appearance.

We knew all along that the contest would be close, but we were not prepared for what happened after election day. We did not know who won for several weeks. At first, it appeared that Stuart won, but his majority began to shrink. It dwindled to five votes. Then the tide shifted to Douglas. There was a report that he rode on the outside of a stage coach from Chicago to Springfield, smoking a cigar, and claiming that his margin over Stuart was 2,000 votes.

The newspapers disputed each other's claims: the *Register* reporting that Douglas won by 150 votes and the *Journal* that Stuart prevailed by 15 votes. Finally, on September 1, the Illinois government officials declared that Stuart's total was 18,254 votes, and Douglas's total was 18,218 votes. Stuart had won by 36 votes.

On September 29, to celebrate Stuart's victory, the Whig Party hosted an enormous barbecue in the afternoon and a formal banquet at night. Some in Springfield were worried that the Whigs would set the town on fire, but the celebrations, while joyous, were not chaotic. At the banquet, Stuart received many toasts from his friends and colleagues. Mine was bittersweet because, while I was delighted he had won a seat in Congress, I would miss his wise counsel. At Stuart and Lincoln, I would be very much on my own.

Stuart's victory took some of the sting out of the loathsome parts of the campaign. We all knew that politics brought out the best and the worst in us. We tended to forgive Douglas his reckless ambition, but it was getting harder.

Late that night I walked by myself toward Speed's store. Over the buildings to the north, the moon was shaded with earthshine, the "old moon in the new moon's arms." I shivered as I felt the first chill of fall in the light breeze. When I turned to the left on Washington Street, I saw a faint shape walking slowly toward me. Gradually, a white-haired old woman, haggard and disheveled, dressed in black, emerged from the shadows. She glanced at me briefly, turned away, and then disappeared into an alley. I was tempted to follow her, but something held me back. There were elderly people without homes in Springfield, and I felt sad that I had hesitated and left her to her ill-starred fate.

Chapter Eight

"A Strong and Sensible Speech"

S tephen Logan called the meeting to order.

Logan was considered by many to be Springfield's best lawyer. Nine years older than I, he grew up in Kentucky and became a circuit county judge shortly after arriving in Illinois. From that time on, he was known as "Judge Logan." Dissatisfied with the pay, he gave up the bench to begin his law career. Logan combined a brilliant legal mind with a remarkable ability to explain the nuances of a case to the jury.

For all his success, Logan paid no attention to his outward appearance. His thick, overgrown hair looked like a bird's nest; his clothes were baggy; and for half the year, he wore a frayed straw hat. He never wore a necktie in court. Perhaps he felt sure enough of himself to dismiss convention, or maybe he just didn't care.

Gathered in the morning at the office of Stuart and Lincoln were Logan, his partner Edward Baker, Cyrus Edwards, Stuart, and I. We were the hastily assembled defense team for Henry B. Truett who was accused of murder.

This was my first major criminal trial since arriving in Springfield a year earlier. People said it was the most sensational case in the town's history. The date of the trial was set for October 8 to allow for passions in Springfield to subside. There would be no opportunity to find impartial jurors in the immediate wake of the crime.

"Gentlemen," declared Logan in his harsh, scratchy voice, "here are the facts as we know them at present. We have them from credible witnesses, one of whom was John Urquhart, our state prosecutor. Urquhart will have to disqualify himself from the case, and, as a result, the prosecuting attorney will be his partner, Stephen Douglas.

"Now to the facts.

"At 8:00 p.m. on the evening of March 7,1838, Dr. Jacob Early was relaxing in the sitting room of the Spotts-wood Hotel in Springfield. Dr. Early had journeyed to Springfield earlier in the day to check on his business interests and to negotiate a railroad contract. It was his practice to stay over at the Spottswood Hotel on these occasions.

"He had enjoyed a hearty supper at the hotel and then adjourned to the sitting room for light conversation with friends. As we all know, Early was an influential Democratic politician, and the topic naturally drifted toward politics.

"The particular subject that engaged the friends was the decision, at the recent Democratic convention in Peoria, to deny Henry Truett renomination for Register of the Land Office in Galena. A second resolution was passed removing him from office immediately. Several of the gentlemen in the sitting room, including Early, had been present at the Peoria convention.

"No sooner had the gentlemen exhausted the topic, than Henry Truett himself entered the room. Surprised by this astonishing coincidence, the men clustered by Early, turned to Truett, and tried to lighten the mood with small talk and jokes.

"One of them said, 'Well, Truett, by the oddest chance, we were just talking about you.'

"Truett replied, 'I hope it was something you would have said to my face.'

"When Truett spied Early sitting comfortably on the sofa, he glowered at him. Several of the men in the room noticed this and were disconcerted by it. Gradually, the crowd thinned out until a handful was left. Early moved to a leather wing chair by the fireplace. He raised his feet onto the fender and opened his copy of the week's *Sangamo Journal.* He was engrossed in his reading, but something must have disturbed him."

Logan stopped. He swept through his hair with his right hand. Stuart looked at him as if he expected a moth to fly out.

Locking his gaze on each of us, Logan asked, "Are there any questions?"

Baker asked if Truett was the son-in-law of William May. Logan nodded. There were no further questions.

"All right, I will continue," he announced.

"When Early looked up, he saw Henry Truett standing next to his chair. He attempted to welcome him with polite conversation.

"'Henry,' he said, 'I didn't expect to see you here to-night.'

"Truett replied, 'Nor did I suspect I would see you.'

"He took a step toward Early and confronted him. His hand was in his pocket, and it covered a large lump.

"Truett said he'd been told that Early wrote the resolution calling for his removal. He asked if this were true.

"Early told him he would respond to the question if Truett revealed the name of the person who had told him.

"Truett shouted that Early was a damned scoundrel and a damned rascal.

"After Early tried to ignore him, he continued to yell that he was a damned hypocrite and a damned coward.

"Early said that if Truett persisted, they would have to settle it elsewhere.

"Truett cried that they would settle it right there.

"He continued his stream of insults, and Early, possibly

realizing the lump in Truett's pocket might be a pistol, sprang up and raised his chair menacingly.

"Truett took a step back in a moment of indecision. Then he glowered at Early once more, plunged his hand into his pocket, pulled out a cocked pistol, and pointed it at him.

"Early held the chair to shield himself from Truett's weapon. Three feet apart, the two swirled around each other with Early trying to keep himself from giving Truett a clean shot. It took a few seconds for Truett to find an opening.

"He pulled the trigger, there was a crash and a shattering bang, and Early fell to the floor.

"The bullet punctured Early's abdomen and cut through his stomach and liver. He was mortally wounded. Truett threw the pistol toward the fireplace and rushed out of the hotel.

"Early suffered for three days and then died.

"Truett was captured, arrested, and jailed. No bail was allowed.

"On March 14, Truett was indicted for the murder of Jacob Early."

When Logan finished, we focused on a point or two from his summary and then began to outline the strategy we would use to defend Henry Truett. This took most of the day. We finished in the late afternoon and agreed to meet again the following morning.

Stuart, Logan, Baker, Edwards, and I met several more times during the summer. Logan took the lead in these discussions. We would frame arguments and give the evidence for them. I began to understand why Logan had earned his reputation. He had a mastery of the details that none of us could match. He delighted in dismantling a hypothesis by demonstrating a flaw in the logic used to support it or by citing a fact we had overlooked.

Logan told me I needed to pay close attention in our meetings because I would probably be giving the closing statement. He must have been impressed with my legal skills and courtroom manner to give me such an important role. It was a major responsibility, and I was a bit nervous about it. What if I failed, and Truett were hanged?

I was never a sound sleeper. I often woke up in the night and had trouble getting back to sleep. Some nights I hardly slept. When that happened, I would dress and then walk through the lonely streets of the town. After an hour or two, I would return home and read for the rest of the night.

To take my mind off my task at the upcoming trial, I overindulged myself in one of my favorite activities in Springfield. With the exception of Douglas, who disdained athletics, the friends who gathered by the fireplace at Speed's store met at a place we called the ball alley to play the game called Fives, in which players hit a ball against the wall using their hands. The ball had to be returned in one bounce. Several of us played at a time.

North of Washington Street on Sixth Street just south of the Illinois State Journal Building was ball alley. We were charged a slight fee for someone to take care of the playing surface. Because the contests were hard fought, the court had to be smoothed afterwards.

On a blistering late afternoon in August, Baker, Speed, Hardin, Matheny, Billy Herndon, and I met at ball alley to play Fives. The team of Speed, Matheny, and I had beaten the others handily in our last outing. They were ready for revenge.

We were sweating profusely as we met at the alley to begin play.

"Whoever gets Lincoln has an unfair advantage," said Baker. "He leaps around like a wounded buffalo, but he does have the agility of an antelope."

"Making excuses already," countered Matheny. "Lincoln may have an edge because he is so tall and has large hands, but he gives it back with all his fouls."

"Yes, Lincoln," said Hardin, "you can't leap all over the court and smash into us. You're an oaf. It's a wonder you haven't given someone a broken arm or leg. We will call the fouls more closely tonight."

"All right, all right," I growled at them. "Let's get started."

The first few points were bitterly contested, but Baker, who was playing particularly well, aimed his shots into the corner where they were impossible to return. In deference to their gibes, I restrained myself from going all out. I felt inhibited and had to find the balance between attacking every ball and moving artfully at key moments. Speed was very good at that, although he didn't play the game with the same passion as I did. Speed was a graceful athlete. I could certainly learn from him.

Baker continued to have a good day, and his team won the first frame. We rallied to win the second one. Because we were drenched with sweat and exhausted, we decided to play an abbreviated third frame. No one gained the advantage. The points were evenly split. We agreed to settle the match with one last point.

Baker served, and running toward the ball, I returned a strong shot to the corner. Getting out of the way, I looked around to see Hardin wallop it back. Speed was able to get to it and made the strategic decision to hit a soft shot. If it worked, we would win, but Billy Herndon sprinted for the wall and made an astonishing save. No one from our team was near, and the ball fell to the ground for a second and third bounce.

We collapsed on the court, worn out by our epic contest. We'd enjoyed the competition, and we'd played well. It was a moment of satisfaction and release.

The summer and early fall flew by, and the trial began on Monday, October 8. The venue was the Sangamon County Circuit Court, which met in the space below the offices of Stuart and Lincoln on Hoffman Row. This was the room to which we had access through the trap door in our office. Judge Jesse B. Thomas Jr. was assigned to preside at the trial.

Because Springfield was still aroused by the killing of Jacob Early, it was a difficult task to find impartial jurors. Attorneys for the prosecution and the defense interviewed more than 400 people to form a jury. Both sides used all of their peremptory challenges, which allowed the dismissal of potential jurors for no stated cause. Finally, on Thursday morning, October 11, a jury was impaneled.

From there, the trial moved swiftly. David M. Woodson, who had just been appointed state's attorney for the First Judicial District, presented the evidence for the prosecution, and Logan summarized the case for the defense. This part of the trial was completed by Thursday night. Friday and Saturday were given over to closing arguments. Douglas was chosen to make the closing statement for the prosecution, and Logan held to his promise that I would give the closing statement for the defense.

Douglas did not speak to the jury until late Saturday afternoon. Although the day had droned on, when Douglas rose to give his statement, the room was silent and expectant.

Although Douglas was my friend, he was not averse to being my antagonist. We'd learned to disagree strenuously in politics and still remain cordial. Now we were giving the closing statements on opposite sides of a murder trial and stretching our bond once more.

In the courtroom, Douglas paced back and forth like a caged tiger. Always eyeing the jury, he moved about furiously waving his arms and alternately raising and lowering his voice. It was not unlike his bearing on the stump.

"Gentlemen of the jury," he began, "we have had a long day. I am much chagrined to keep you from your guesthouses and your taverns any longer, but we do have business before us which we must conclude. I can reassure you that this phase of our work will not be onerous. It should not consume any more of your precious time than it takes my lanky friend, the assistant counsel for the defense, to do the three hop. Gentlemen, I am told he can do it in 40.2 seconds.

"The trail of evidence that leads us to the door of the defendant Henry Truett is so firmly established and so clearly demonstrated that it cannot but erase any shred of reasonable doubt that could possibly trouble you. Nay, I shall simply review the facts which the prosecution lay before you yesterday, and my job is done. For the conclusion, gentlemen, can be only that the defendant, Henry Truett, is guilty of the murder of our beloved friend and colleague, Dr. Jacob Early.

"First and foremost, two witnesses have sworn before you that they saw Truett remove a pistol from his pocket and, from a range of three feet, shoot Jacob Early in the abdomen causing his death three days later.

"Next, in a declaration given shortly before his death, and a declaration that Judge Thomas, over the objection of the defense, ruled admissible, Jacob Early stated that Truett initiated the attack upon him without provocation.

"Next, the witnesses stated that upon entering the Spottswood Hotel, Henry Truett hung his overcoat on the hotel coatrack, removed a pistol from the overcoat, cocked the pistol, and placed it in his pocket. He then entered the sitting room.

"Next, Truett confronted Jacob Early in the sitting room with a malign expression on his face. So sinister was this look that the witnesses were deeply troubled.

"Next, in the course of their altercation, Henry Truett removed the pistol from his pocket and threatened Jacob Early. Dr. Early tried to defend himself by raising his chair as a shield. Truett turned in a circular motion seeking a clear shot. Dr. Early continued to defend himself, but Truett found the opening he sought, pulled the trigger, and shot Dr. Early.

"Next, upon shooting Jacob Early, Truett threw the murder weapon across the room and rushed out into the night. The villain fled from the scene of his crime. He eluded his pursuers for a day and was finally captured, arrested, and locked in jail. Per my order, he was not allowed to be free on bail. The defense has portrayed him as having suffered greatly over the past seven months of incarceration, but should a dangerous and unhinged criminal be allowed to roam our streets at will?

"Finally, gentlemen, what was Henry Truett's motive? It is as clear as it possibly can be. It's as old as time, as old as Cain and Abel. Henry Truett could not face the truth about himself. God rejected Cain's offering and accepted Abel's. What did Cain do? He was very wroth, and rose up against Abel his brother and slew him. Henry Truett could not accept the judgment of his colleagues that he had not performed his duties properly. Not only had they seen fit to deny him the opportunity for further service, but they voted to terminate him immediately. This was done, and for him, 'sin lieth at the door.' Because he was wroth, he slew Dr. Jacob Early.

"Gentlemen, there can no doubt that Henry Truett is guilty. His crime was premeditated in the furnace of his rage, his envy, and his pride. He could not suppress these primordial and sinful urges to murder the man whom he was certain had authored his demise.

You have heard the witnesses, you have heard the evidence, you have heard our summary, and now you have heard my conclusion. All these parts bring us to the whole: that your duty is to convict Henry Truett of the murder of Dr. Jacob Early."

Douglas finished with a flourish, and there were audible gasps of admiration for his effort. I had to admit that he spoke powerfully and eloquently. He threw himself down in his chair, mopped his brow with his handkerchief, and breathed heavily. However confident I was of my ability to match him, when he finished, my heart raced and my stomach tightened, knowing I would be speaking next.

In speaking to an audience or in arguing a case in court, it always took me a minute or two to feel comfortable. My voice tightened, causing it to sound higher; my hands cut through the air with nervous energy; and my pace was too fast. Gradually I eased into my rhythm, and I felt comfortable on the stump or in court.

"The assistant counsel for the defense," Judge Thomas called, prodding me to come forward and begin my remarks.

I rose from my chair, stretched briefly, and walked toward the jury box. It relaxed me to nod at the jurors as if I were introducing myself. I knew five of them, and they acknowledged me by a nod or the trace of a smile.

"Gentlemen of the jury, as the associate counsel for the prosecution has told us, the hour is late. I will do my duty, but I will be brief.

"Our five days of deliberation—this whole case—can be pared down to one word: intent.

"What was Henry Truett's intent as he confronted Jacob Early in the sitting room of the Spottswood Hotel on the evening of March 7?

"Yes, gentlemen, Henry Truett brought a pistol with him to the Spottswood Hotel, but, no, gentlemen, Truett did not intend to kill Jacob Early with it. It was Truett's practice to carry a pistol with him every day—not just the evening of March 7.

"Yes, Henry Truett confronted Early when unexpectedly he encountered him that evening.

"Yes, he had a hateful expression on his face when he spoke to Early.

"Yes, he demanded to know if Early was the author of the resolution that disgraced him.

"Yes, he insulted Early.

"Yes, he reached into his pocket, removed his pistol, and pointed it at Early.

"The witnesses told us they saw this. What they didn't and couldn't tell us is why they saw it.

"Gentlemen of the jury, have you known your friends and colleagues to betray and censure you? Have you known the loss of your honor? This is what Henry Truett endured. That is why Henry Truett confronted Jacob Early, stared at him hatefully, insulted him, and pointed his pistol at him.

"What happened next?

"Jacob Early rose from his chair, took hold of it, and raised it to a level from which he could strike Truett with it. He threatened Truett with what could be construed—certainly in those circumstances—as a deadly weapon. He became the aggressor.

"And what did Henry Truett do next?

"He took a step backward.

"Why?

"To protect himself from an attack by Jacob Early.

"What might have happened had Early retreated one step?

"But he didn't.

"They circled each other, and Henry Truett, believing his life was threatened by Jacob Early, shot him in self-defense.

"Henry Truett never intended to kill Jacob Early. There was no malice aforethought. There was no premeditation. When he came upon Early in the hotel sitting room, an encounter he did not expect, the rage he had felt for months surfaced and caused him to menace and threaten Jacob Early.

"If you or I had been wronged as Henry Truett thought he was, what would you or I have done?

"We would have confronted our betrayer and assailed him. This was Henry Truett's intent. He did not intend to kill Jacob Early.

"Gentlemen of the jury, you will now receive your instructions from the judge, retire for as long as necessary, and return with a verdict. In your hands is the life of Henry Truett. Unless you believe, beyond the shadow of a doubt, he is guilty of murder and should forfeit his life for that offense, I ask that you acquit him of the charge."

When I finished, I returned to the defense table, sat down in my chair, took several deep breaths, and rested quietly. Had I saved Henry Truett's life? Probably not, but I had done my best.

Logan reached over and shook my hand warmly.

Judge Thomas gave the jury their charge, and they walked out the front door and up the steps to our office directly above. That was the room chosen for the jury's deliberations.

Stuart, Baker, Logan, Edwards, and I ate a late dinner at the Crown and Cock. Douglas and the prosecution were eating at a nearby table. After two hours, we were alerted that the jury had reached a verdict, and we all rushed over to the courtroom.

When everyone was settled, Judge Thomas asked the defendant to rise.

To the foreman of the jury, he asked, "Have you reached a verdict?"

"Yes, your Honor, we have reached a verdict."

Judge Thomas asked, "Gentlemen of the jury, how

find you the defendant, Henry B. Truett, on the charge of murder, guilty or not guilty?"

"Not guilty," said the foreman.

I was stunned. I had anticipated a guilty verdict. The others had learned to mask their faces at the rendering of a verdict, but I was surprised and elated, and I'm sure it showed.

For several weeks after the trial, I received congratulations on my closing statement. Since I knew in advance that it would be my responsibility, I had prepared thoroughly for it, both before and at the trial. Logan told me I had given a "strong and sensible speech."

His words meant more to me than any others.

Oddly, at this moment of accomplishment, my feelings of sadness and melancholy returned. How strange it was that at moments when others celebrated, I sometimes could not. As far as I could tell, there was no particular event or circumstance that caused this. It may be that, although I had helped save a man's life, I wondered whether justice had been served.

As I walked the streets, I felt cheerless and dispirited. Images of my mother and my sister, who died when I was a boy in Indiana, drifted through my mind and haunted me. I thought of Annie, and of our love for each other in New Salem, before she died. My midnight walks, often by moonlight, eased the despair enough for me to sleep. Speed told me my face betrayed my gloom. He said he sometimes felt the same, and his remedy was to plunge into his work. He also told me to read deeper into the poetry of Byron. I resolved to do that as well.

Chapter Nine

"WHO ARE YOU BECOMING?"

The year 1840 brought the presidential election we all anticipated. As Stuart had predicted, the prospects for the Whig candidate were strong. Passing over Henry Clay, the first Whig national convention nominated the military hero, General William Henry Harrison. His opponent was the incumbent Democratic president, Martin Van Buren.

The issues in Stuart's race against Douglas for the congressional seat foreshadowed the issues in the presidential campaign. Key among them was the country's economic crisis. The Democrats could not hide from the action that caused it: Jackson's refusal to recharter the Second Bank of the United States. It unleashed the wave of economic instability that crashed over the Van Buren presidency. Nothing he did could stop it. In the election of 1840, he would have to run on his record.

I became the leader of the Whig campaign for Harrison in Illinois. For eight months, I spoke for Harrison across the state. Many of us were involved, which meant I could still attend to the cases in which the firm of Stuart and Lincoln agreed to represent clients.

My standard stump speech emphasized the Whig platform: reestablishing the national bank, enacting a protective tariff, and supporting internal improvements. I portrayed the Whigs as the party for the rising man.

One Whig-Democrat debate during the Harrison campaign took place in the courtroom below our office. My friend, Edward Baker, was speaking for the Whigs. He was a formidable presence on the stump and a passionate orator. It was Baker that Speed had cast as the lion in our play because the part was nothing but roaring.

I happened to be upstairs writing the declaration on a debt collection case. When Baker started to speak, I discarded my papers, took my feet off the table, and rose from my chair. I walked softly over to the trap door. Just below it was the dais where the speaker stood when he addressed the crowd. I lay down on the floor and stealthily opened the trap door. I could see Baker's head bobbing just below me, hear his rapid delivery, and watch him waving his arms furiously as he attacked the Democrats.

He cried, "wherever there is a land office there is a Democratic newspaper to defend its corruptions."

This was too much for the brother of the *Illinois Register*'s editor. The faithful sibling yelled, "Pull him down," and charged at Baker.

Baker turned to defend himself as the crowd jumped to its feet and urged on the attacker.

I didn't hesitate and started to lower myself through the trap door. I think the pair of dangling legs stunned the attacker and crowd into silence. I dropped to the floor, steadied myself, and grabbed a stone water pitcher that happened to be on the podium.

I yelled, "I will break this pitcher over the head of the first man who lays hands on Baker."

Breathing heavily for a moment, I calmed myself and told them firmly, "Hold on, gentlemen, this is the land of free speech. Mr. Baker has a right to speak and ought to be heard. I am here to protect him. And no man shall take him from this stand if I can prevent it."

This quieted the crowd, and Baker continued vigorously.

Once the campaign started in earnest, the Illinois Whig speakers for Harrison fanned out into the state.

Chief among the Democratic speakers supporting Van
Buren was Stephen Douglas. With his relentless energy,
his speaking engagements carried him into every corner
of the state. When we overlapped in the legislature, we
had strenuously opposed each other on the issues. It was
inevitable that we would face each other on the stump.

In March, we met in Jacksonville for a debate.

We expected Douglas to make the charge that the
Whigs were abolitionists. In a Van Buren campaign
paper, we were reviled for wanting to place the government, "into the hands of a set of fanatics, who boldly
proclaim that they would sacrifice their country, its
liberties, its honor, and its glory, TO MAKE THE NE-
GRO THE EQUAL OF THE WHITE MAN."

While I believed slavery was unjust, I also believed abolition doctrine increased rather than abated slavery's evils.

I was ready to counter that the real abolitionist was
Van Buren. In the New York convention of 1821, he
voted to allow suffrage for free Negroes.

I decided to set a trap for Douglas. William Holland's biography of Van Buren included the account of
his support for Negro suffrage. I would take my copy of
Holland's book with me to the debate.

Despite the cold, gray March weather, a large crowd
attended the event. For Douglas, it was a hometown
crowd. He was at his bombastic best. With vigor and
vitriol, he castigated Harrison as an abolitionist. When
he finished his standard denunciation of the Whig platform, it was my turn to respond.

I began with my case for electing Harrison and by
defending the Whig program for the next four years.

When I finished the main portion of my speech, I turned to Douglas and recounted the facts surrounding our claim that Van Buren had supported Negro suffrage in 1821. I took out my copy of Holland's biography.

Slowly, and with emphasis, I read the pages from the book. The crowd quieted. As I continued to read, they murmured anxiously.

Douglas stood up and rushed over to me. He came up to the top of my chest. With his face flushed, he yelled out, "It is a damned forgery!"

I held him off and retorted, "No, my friend, I'm afraid it's not."

There were roars of derision from the crowd, but also cries of, "It's so, it's so."

With a look of satisfaction, he bellowed at me, "Lies, lies, all infernal, damnable lies!"

He grabbed the book from my hands, threw it out into the crowd, and then shouted, "Any man who would write such a book and send it out to the great West, expecting that it would advance Van Buren's interest, is a damned fool."

Several weeks later, I returned to the stump to debate Col. Dick Taylor, a noisy Democrat who was a fancy dresser. He modeled his stump style after Douglas and spoke passionately when attacking the Whigs as aristocrats and elitists.

While Col. Taylor was pontificating, I had an idea. I moved delicately toward him, and when I was within range, I plucked the corner of his vest. It unbuttoned, and out popped his ruffled shirt, two large gold watches with seals, and his gold watch chains.

The crowd, both Democrats and Whigs, roared with laughter. The flustered Taylor continued, but there were no more remarks about Whig elitists and aristocrats.

On July 20, a hot, muggy day in Springfield, it was my turn to campaign for Harrison and debate Judge Jesse B. Thomas, a Democrat who was speaking for Van Buren.

Thomas was incensed that we had written anonymous letters to the newspapers that appeared to come from him. He had been attacked for what he had supposedly written. He vilified me as the leader of this dirty trick and called me a coward who hid behind anonymity. As he continued and concluded with his recital of the case for Van Buren's reelection, I was beginning to simmer and finally to boil.

When I strode up to the podium and began speaking, I did not hold back.

I began by saying that as a humble member of the legislature, I could never puff myself up to the magnitude of my eminent colleague, Judge Thomas. I said it reminded me of the frog in the fable.

When the ox trod on the young frogs, one escaped to tell his mother how big it was. She puffed herself up saying, "Was it as big as this?" When the little frog replied, "Oh, a great deal bigger," in her folly, she puffed herself up even more. Finally the little frog said, "I'm afraid you'll burst before you can reach even half its size." His vain mother puffed once more and burst into thin air.

I said I had learned that lesson and would refrain from such foolishness.

At this point, rather than repeating the regular Whig arguments for Harrison's election, I decided to assail Judge Thomas with the inconsistencies of his political career.

And then I did something I had never done from the stump before. Over the years, my friends had told me I was a superb mimic. It was true. I couldn't resist this chance to humiliate Thomas. I strutted around the platform imitating his walk, and I mocked his gestures and the motions of his body. I chose lines from his speech and mimicked the peculiarities of his voice and accent. I ridiculed his delivery. The crowd adored it. They called for more, and I obliged them.

Thomas turned pale, and etched in his face was the horror of what was unfolding.

I did not stop. I was caught up in the frenzy of the crowd. I was on stage and loving it.

I looked over at Thomas and to my surprise, I saw him weeping. Here was a grown man crying at his own foibles brought to life in a political forum.

That evening when I returned to the store, Speed was sitting by the fireplace finishing his supper. I sat down and relaxed in the chair next to him. He seemed preoccupied and did not look at me.

"We took Thomas down today," I began.

He said nothing.

"Were you there?"

He did not reply.

"Are you all right?" I asked.

"I was there," he said quietly.

"Then you saw it."

"I did," he said quietly, putting his hands over his face.

"Wasn't it grand?" I said triumphantly.

"I was there," he said with an edge in his voice.

I hesitated and then said, "What do you mean by this?"

"Lincoln, what I saw you do today was not only mean

and hurtful—it was merciless. It was not slasher-gaff, and you know I sometimes question that. What you did today frightens me."

"Speed, you don't understand. It's politics."

"You've said that before, and if you don't understand, you are blind to how cruel you were."

"But he called me a coward."

"And why did he call you that?"

"Because he was furious about the letters."

"And who wrote those letters?

"I did."

"And he had no right to be angry?"

I said nothing.

"Thomas is our friend," he said. "He is a respected judge. You have argued cases before him. He presided at Truett's trial. He comes to our evening gatherings. He is a Democrat, but when he comes here, as you know, that is forgiven. You had no right to treat him that way."

"He needs a tougher skin."

"You were over a line, and if you don't see that, you are not the person I thought you were."

"I enjoyed it."

"At the expense of someone else's suffering? Who are you becoming?"

I glared at him.

"Lincoln, you cannot hide from what you did. You must apologize to him."

The following day, I had breakfast with my friends. They were subdued, and the conversation was muted.

Finally Baker looked at me and said, "Lincoln, before you joined us, we all agreed to tell you how we felt about yesterday. We were surprised and dismayed by what you did to Thomas. We all know that politics can be vicious and ugly, but what you did yesterday was wrong. There are some lines we respect, and you crossed one of them yesterday. You must apologize to Thomas."

When an editorial in the *Illinois State Register* condemned my attack on Thomas and claimed that many of my fellow Whigs were in agreement, I began to realize that Speed and the others might be right.

What caused me to cross that line? I hadn't intended to humiliate Thomas, but that is what happened. When the crowd cheered my mimicry, I felt a connection to an audience I had never felt before. The more I ridiculed him, the more frenzied they became. The power was intoxicating, and I yielded my judgment to the collective will of the actor and the audience. Speed was right. It was frightening.

It was time for me to apologize to Thomas.

The next day, I met with him in his courtroom. We sat in the two chairs by the small table for the prosecuting attorneys.

Thomas had a square face with a kindly countenance. He was a man of few words, and I began our conversation.

"Judge," I said awkwardly, "I want to apologize."

"Yes," he said slowly.

"I was caught up in the frenzy of the moment. My friends have helped me to see that I was over a line."

"Yes, you were. You should have known it yourself."

"Politics can be cruel and ugly."

"It doesn't have to be."

"I should have known better."

"Yes, you should have, but no hard feelings, Lincoln. I appreciate your apology. I have known you to be an honorable man. I was surprised by your hostility. That's not something I would have expected from you."

Although I could barely speak, I uttered a few words of thanks, looked him in the eye, shook his hand, and then walked out into the morning sunlight.

In November, the voters decided the contest between Harrison and Van Buren on the substantive issues. Harrison won easily with a 234-60 electoral vote victory over Van Buren. Nationally the Whigs rejoiced, and Illinois Whigs joined in the celebrations but for one hitch: Van Buren won only seven states, but one of them was Illinois.

Chapter Ten

And What of Marrying at All?

After the death of Ann Rutledge in the summer of 1835, there was a part of me that remained dormant. A year later in New Salem, I tried to kindle an interest in Mary Owens, but the flame was not there for either of us.

My friends were all young men, and I often felt uncomfortable around women who were my age. I gave little thought to marriage, instead immersing myself in studying and eventually practicing the law. When I won a seat in the legislature, politics became my passion. Although some of my Springfield friends were starting to court young women, I was not interested and held back.

During the Harrison campaign, however, events took place which reawakened that slumbering side of me.

Once Springfield became the state capital, the legislature met from late November through March. "Legislative winter" as it came to be known was a time of intense social activity. The town hosted rising young lawyers who were members of the legislature or trying cases in the Illinois Supreme Court or the federal District Court of Illinois. Joining them for social events were young women who lived in Springfield or who came to town from afar for the fun and gaiety of the cotillions, dances, and parties. It was not uncommon for young women searching for husbands to visit relatives during the "legislative winter."

In the winter of 1839–40, my friends and I eased into a group of young men and women who joined each other for social occasions. Eventually, we were dubbed the "Springfield Coterie." Our most ambitious gala was a cotillion that 16 young men, including me, hosted at the American House, the grand hotel near the central square. There was live music, dancing, and a bounty of exotic food and fine wine. Political speeches were encouraged, but they were expected to be short and amusing.

When it snowed, the young men and women of the Coterie went for sleigh rides at Hardin's farm in Jacksonville.
After a day of outdoor frolic, we relaxed in front of a roaring fire. Speed, Hardin, Baker, Douglas, and I were joined
by James Conkling, Lyman Trumbull, Orville Browning,
and James Shields. Browning was now married, and his
wife Eliza became my confidante. The young women
whom we saw most often were Mercy Levering, Catherine
Bergen, Julia Jayne, and Mary Todd. Miss Todd was staying in Springfield with her older sister, Elizabeth Edwards.

Elizabeth and Ninian Edwards owned a large house in
a part of Springfield called Aristocracy Hill. There were
no real hills in Springfield, but it was a small rise southwest
of the town square. Near the Edwards were the estates of
the Levering and Jayne families. Members of the Coterie were frequently invited to informal gatherings at the
Edwards' house.

Ever since coming to Springfield, I couldn't quite overcome an awkwardness I felt at social affairs. It may have
come from my background, but it was also part of my
nature. It must have been apparent to everyone. With their
familiarity that flowed into social grace, I couldn't match
my friends' polish and ease at our gatherings.

They were all good dancers, and I was miserable at it.
Their musical instrument was the violin and their dance
the waltz; my instrument was the fiddle and my dance
the country strut. My height was no help. Conkling said
I looked like "old Father Jupiter bending down from the
clouds to see what was going on."

Although I excelled at the Fives game, it was because
of my reach and range and sheer willingness to fling
myself around the court—not from fluid movement and
athletic form.

Speed was familiar with Washington Irving's tale about the headless horseman. He read parts of it to me from time to time. He couldn't resist gently torturing me with Irving's description of the schoolmaster, Ichabod Crane.

"He was tall, but exceedingly lank," Speed read archly, "with narrow shoulders, long arms and legs, hands that dangled a mile out of his sleeves, feet that might have served for shovels, and his whole frame most loosely hung together. His head was small, and flat at top, with huge ears, large green glassy eyes, and a long snipe nose, so that it looked like a weathercock, perched upon his spindle neck, to tell which way the wind blew."

"It's you!" Speed would cry with glee. "The only thing that's wrong is that he has a small head, but the nose is right, the feet are right, and so is everything else. The name doesn't quite do it. I don't think you'd go anywhere in politics if you were Ichabod Lincoln. It's one of those eastern names, not from the Old Testament, like yours."

It was at the soirees at the Edwards' house that I began to notice Miss Todd. She was short, a little plump, and quite pretty. She was someone whose personality sparkled in her looks. Always animated, she was the center of attention. Speed was taken with her, but he'd heard that she was sweet on Douglas. I had to admit she and Douglas made a perfect pair. They were the same height, and as they glided together on the dance floor, they looked like courting doves.

A soiree at the Edwards' house could be a party for over a hundred guests, or it could be a more informal gathering for the Springfield Coterie. I was more comfortable at the smaller affairs where Mary Todd and her two closest friends, Mercy Levering and Julia Jayne, chatted amiably with a wide circle of male acquaintances. The handsome and charming Speed was one of their favorites.

The favored place for more intimate conversations was the parlor. It was a warm, cozy room with a marble fireplace, above which hung several family portraits. The furniture was so fancy that it was considered decorative art. Two identical sofas in the parlor were among the finest pieces in the house. They were black with horsehair upholstery on mahogany frames. For comfort, they were unmatched.

At a late afternoon gathering in the spring of 1840, I was wandering abstractedly through the Edwards' house when I observed Speed and Mary Todd conversing easily on one of the horsehair sofas. They were the only couple in the parlor.

Speed saw me turning to walk away and called loudly, "Lincoln, come here and join us."

I moved toward the receiving room where most of our friends were congregating.

Speed jumped from the sofa, rushed toward me, and pulled me by the arm. He beckoned me to join him and Miss Todd. I could not refuse without seeming impolite. He led me into the parlor and motioned for me to sit beside Miss Todd. He sat on the other side of her.

"Lincoln," he said to me, "Have you met Miss Todd?"

Without looking at her, I replied, "We are familiar with each other."

"Well, we may be familiar with each other, but nary a word has passed between us," said Miss Todd airily.

"We can certainly take care of that," said Speed.

He turned to the lovely young woman next to him and said, "Miss Todd, Mr. Lincoln is a rising politician in the

Whig Party. He is their floor leader in the house. He is also becoming known as one of our most diligent and able lawyers."

"Yes, I have heard that," she said. "My cousin Stuart chose him as his partner, and he thinks well of Mr. Lincoln."

I looked at her and nodded in appreciation.

She smiled and asked "Mr. Lincoln, what do you think of General Harrison's chances in the general election?"

"Why how coincidental of you, Miss Todd," I replied. "I have just written to Stuart about that very topic."

I looked at the floor to concentrate, and then, since I had written the letter the day before, the words came to me. I looked toward the fireplace and quoted from my letter: "You know I am never sanguine, but I believe we will carry the state. The chance for doing so appears to me 25% better than it did for you to beat Douglas. Our Irish blacksmith Gregory is for Harrison."

Speed could not resist and teased me by saying, "Lincoln, surely you can talk to Miss Todd without having to quote from your correspondence."

I felt my face grow warm, and I turned away from them both.

Miss Todd saved us by saying, "Mr. Lincoln can speak for himself. I have heard him several times from the stump. He does not lack for eloquence."

"Thank you, Miss Todd," I replied.

She added, "And it is indeed good news that the Irish blacksmith Gregory is for Harrison. One would expect a common laborer to be a Jacksonian—and hence for Van Buren. My cousin will be delighted to hear that."

At the next soiree at the Edwards' house, I was wandering aimlessly through the large, opulent rooms, when Miss

Todd happened to look in my direction, broke off a conversation with Mercy Levering, and approached me.

I was surprised by this because at a party shortly after our first meeting, I gathered the courage to tell Miss Todd I wanted to dance with her in the worst way. It was time for me at least to try. She was delighted with my offer. I chose a waltz because I could at least maneuver around the floor counting 1-2-3...1-2-3. I held her left hand and stretched my right arm around her waist. She placed her left hand on my shoulder. The music began, and we were in trouble from the start. First, it was awkward because I was too tall, and she was too short; next, I just couldn't move to the rhythm of the music, and twice I stepped on her toes. When we were finished, she thanked me and told Julia Jayne, who was standing next to us, that I had, in fact, danced with her in the worst way.

"Why, Mr. Lincoln," she said pleasantly, "Won't you accompany me to the parlor?"

I nodded my assent.

She took my hand and led me. There was no one on either of the sofas. She chose the one nearest to the fireplace and bade me sit. I did, and after an awkward few moments, she asked, "I understand you've been giving more speeches for Harrison. How have they been received?"

"It is good of you to ask," I replied. "Most of our crowds are Whigs, and, of course, they are fiercely partisan, but our reception in Democratic strongholds has not been hostile. They are listening, which is quite unusual."

She continued, "The Democrats have also been ruined by the depression. Do you think they will turn to the Whigs for help?"

"I believe they will."

"Do you think we can stabilize our currency so we don't have to depend on specie?"

I was impressed by her question. It showed an understanding of the political and economic issues of the day.

"Yes, I do," I replied.

"And part of the problem was restricting the sale of public lands to specie?"

"Yes, it was."

"Jackson's Specie Circular?"

"Yes. Miss Todd, you are interested in these questions, and you understand the issues. I am impressed."

"You need not be, Mr. Lincoln. I was raised in a family where politics was our supper conversation. Henry Clay is a friend of my father's, and he often dined with us."

This was the first of our conversations in the Edwards' house parlor. Through the late spring and early summer, we met there with greater frequency.

The Todds came from a prominent family in Lexington, Kentucky. The patriarch was a founder of the town. His son Robert, Mary's father, was a successful businessman and politician, and he married Eliza Parker, the daughter of another powerful Lexington family. Eliza died of a fever following the birth of their eighth child. Robert remarried a younger woman shortly after his wife's death, and Betsey Todd gave birth to seven more children.

Though it was unusual for a young woman, Mary had been in school until she was 18. Her first school was run by an Episcopal priest, Dr. John Ward, who believed in scholarly education for young women. At her next school, Madame Mentelle's boarding school, she learned to speak fluent French. Although her family lived nearby, she boarded at the school for four years.

When she came to Springfield, Mary quickly attracted the interest of all the eligible young men. She was lively, cultured, and charming. Conkling called her the "very creature of excitement."

There was a story about her that caught everyone's attention. Just a few weeks earlier, she and Mercy Levering, in full finery, walked from Aristocracy Hill to the town square using wood shingles to prop themselves up in the spring mud. They reached their destination without mishap, but were not successful returning. Covered in mud, Mary hailed a drayman to drive them home. Mercy, believing no proper young lady would do such a thing, refused the offer. Not so Mary Todd. Rather than being scandalized, she relished her ride on a delivery man's cart through the streets of Aristocracy Hill with her lower half caked in mud.

One member of the Coterie even wrote a poem celebrating Mary's adventure of riding home on the drayman's cart.

> As I walked out on Monday last
> A wet and muddy day
> 'Twas there I saw a pretty lass
> A riding on a dray.
> Quoth I sweet lass, what do you there
> Said she good lack a day
> I had no coach to take me home
> So I'm riding on a dray.
> Up flew windows, up popped heads
> To see this Lady gay
> In silken cloak and feathers white
> A riding on a dray.
> At length arrived at Edwards' gate

> Hart back the usual way
> And taking out the iron pin
> He rolled her off the dray.

As our conversations in the Edwards' house parlor continued, we discovered that we had many common pursuits. Above all was our love of poetry. Mary was familiar with Burns, Byron, and Shakespeare. She read Burns's poems with feeling, and she appreciated his sharp wit. She loved to hear me perform "Holy Willie's Prayer."

On one occasion I recited the lines from a stanza at the beginning of Byron's "Childe Harold's Pilgrimage":

> Yet oft-times in his maddest mirthful mood
> Strange pangs would flash along Childe
> Harold's brow,
> As if the memory of some deadly feud
> Or disappointed passion lurk'd below:
> But this none knew, nor haply cared to know;
> For his was not that open, artless soul
> That feels relief by bidding sorrow flow,
> Nor sought he friend to counsel or condole,
> Whate'er this grief mote be, which he could
> not control.

When I concluded, she asked me, "Is that you, Mr. Lincoln? You do not seem sanguine this afternoon."

"No, Miss Todd," I replied, "it is to my friend Speed that I owe my love of Byron. He is the one with whom I can 'counsel or condole.'"

"Fortunate you are, Mr. Lincoln, if that is true."

I had become completely at ease gazing at her pretty blue eyes and her pleasing face with its lovely complexion.

In June, I began to campaign in earnest for Harrison. I had to balance my political engagements with my law practice.

On May 23, in a case on the Eighth Circuit in DeWitt County, Douglas and I were co-counsels for the defense. Spencer Turner was charged with the murder of Matthew K. Martin. We were able to gain Turner an acquittal because the deceased had "kept himself in a state of intoxication and exposure in rain and inclemency of the weather on the night previous to his death," and because Turner's blow had been struck in self-defense.

With the constant travel, I had less time for the social events in Springfield. Elizabeth Edwards encouraged me to visit with Mary whenever I wished. I think she saw me as a rising man.

Mary disclosed her plans to visit relatives in Missouri for the summer. We would not see each other for two months. We decided to write as often as we could.

Perhaps because we were physically removed from each other, Mary and I became more familiar in our correspondence. We were faithful to each other by writing back the day we received a letter. I felt myself growing closer to her.

In one letter, she told me that she was introduced to the grandson of Patrick Henry, a young man whom her family assessed as a splendid match. She wrote, "Much as I was taken with him, I love him not, and my hand will never be given where my heart is not."

When I realized I was heartened by what I read, I knew my feelings for Mary Todd were deepening.

When Mary returned in early September, we resumed our trysts in the Edwards' parlor. Somehow our correspondence created a deepening bond between us. We had only a few days together because I was embarking on a speaking tour that would continue for most of the fall. Writing would be harder as I would be traveling to so many different cities and towns in Illinois.

Two years earlier, I had written to Eliza Browning in jest, "I have now come to the conclusion never again to think of marrying, and for this reason, I can never be satisfied with anyone who would be blockhead enough to have me."

Now there was someone who just might be blockhead enough to have me. This was still a surprise.

She seemed so taken with Douglas. They were always animated and aglow in each other's company. He was the most ambitious and successful of us. Mary told her friends she would marry a future president. Surely she was thinking of Douglas. It looked as if she would catch him, and he seemed quite content with it.

Why had she taken an interest in me? Surely the difference in our backgrounds and my lack of social grace would deter her. What of my temperament—alternately sanguine and melancholic—would it not repel her? Surely she'd prefer any of her handsome suitors compared to someone with my homely looks. Wouldn't I be seen as someone looking to improve my social position by marrying her? Surely she'd learned that I was just as happy away from home as I was at home.

And what of marrying at all? Only once had I known someone dear enough to love, and that was long past. Now that I was older, I had become self-sufficient. At 31, I was well past the age when most men married. Perhaps I was right when I wrote to Eliza Browning. Perhaps it was best not to think of marrying.

Chapter Eleven

THE DOUBTS BEGAN

In early September, I prepared to travel throughout mid-Illinois taking cases in the towns and villages of the 8th Judicial Circuit. Prior to my departure, Mary and I walked together each afternoon. We marched through the streets of Springfield toward the gentle fields just outside town. We discovered a grassy knoll or a large, shady oak tree where we could sit and enjoy the lovely weather and each other's company. A sunny spell settled over the prairie, and, as we inhaled the crisp early fall air, our spirits brightened. I had taken to calling her Molly after the name her close friends gave her.

During these pleasant escapes, we alternately engaged in animated chatter or quiet reflection. I do not remember how the idea of marriage first surfaced in our conversations. I believe it was when we were reciting poetry to each other, and Molly chose one of Shakespeare's sonnets.

> Let me not to the marriage of true minds,
> Admit impediments. Love is not love
> Which alters when it alteration finds,
> Or bends with the remover to remove.
> O no! it is an ever-fixed mark
> That looks on tempests and is never shaken;
> It is the star to every wand'ring bark,
> Whose worth's unknown, although his height be taken.
> Love's not Time's fool, though rosy lips and cheeks
> Within his bending sickle's compass come;
> Love alters not with his brief hours and weeks,
> But bears it out even to the edge of doom.
> If this be error and upon me prov'd,
> I never writ, nor no man ever lov'd.

After her recitation, the subject arose quite naturally.

"Do you ever think of marrying, Mr. Lincoln?" she asked.

"But, Molly, who would be blockhead enough to have me?"

"Whatever do you mean by that?"

"You know I'm not as handsome as Conkling, Speed, Baker, or Hardin. You told your friends I danced in the worst way. You want to marry a president, and that will never be me. And I enjoy being alone."

"Oh, Mr. Lincoln, you are not kind to yourself. If any of that were an impediment, it could be changed. Do you not realize that from some angles you are handsome?"

"But to marry, I should have to be very much in love."

"Will it be hard for you to love someone?"

"It wasn't once, but that was long ago."

"Perhaps it can be true again."

On our last afternoon before I set out to ride the circuit, we chose an idyllic spot by the Sangamon River. Under a large sycamore tree for shade and support, we sat together on the riverbank and watched the current moving leisurely past us. Moving slowly, a pair of ducks swam upriver.

In the afternoon sunshine, we both felt quite mellow. Our thoughts drifted along much like the first fallen leaves floating past us. They were still green but flecked with brown edges. But for an occasional soft breeze, it was so still.

It was on this afternoon that Molly and I became engaged to marry. She led me to the choice, and I made it willingly. We had been seeing each other steadily since the early spring. Molly's sister Elizabeth had fostered the match, although her husband Ninian was not as enthusiastic because he saw our different backgrounds as a hindrance.

Molly was a lovely companion. She was highly intelligent, passionate about politics, a staunch advocate for Whig causes, a devotee of the newspapers, a lively presence at social events, and a thoughtful observer of people. She was ideally suited to be a politician's wife.

And she believed in me. She could have chosen any of the fashionable young men in Springfield. When I asked her why she had not chosen Douglas, she replied once again that she could not give her hand where her heart was not. I protested that Douglas was far ahead of me in the race of ambition. She reminded me of the fable of the tortoise and the hare. I told her what an elegant couple she and Douglas had made. She told me to look beneath the surface for the truth. It was the same lesson I had tried to teach Speed about Macbeth.

She loved the theater, music, and literature. It had not been since Jack Kelso introduced me to Burns and Shakespeare in New Salem, that I had found a friend to share my love of language and poetry. She was so cultivated and refined. She was right: where I had rough edges, I could change.

When we made our pledge to marry, we did not decide when we would be wed. We decided to keep our engagement secret. We would allow no one the chance to argue that we were not right for each other. As we left our sacred spot that afternoon, we sealed our love with our first kiss.

I thought I knew myself, but subsequent events showed I did not.

For the next eight weeks, I was riding my horse from

town to town on the circuit. I did not return to Springfield until mid-November.

Shortly after my return, a surprise awaited all the young men of Springfield. Cyrus Edwards, a prominent Whig politician and lawyer from Alton, brought his 18-year-old daughter Matilda with him to Springfield. After her arrival, Ninian and Elizabeth Edwards invited Matilda, who was Ninian's cousin, to stay with them for the Springfield social season.

Matilda Edwards was a revelation. She was a classic beauty—tall, blond, and willowy. Not only were her looks striking, but she was known for her gentle temperament and sweetness of heart. Molly, who shared her room with Matilda at the Edwards' house, said, "A lovelier girl I have never seen."

She was the epitome of grace and charm. Within days, the young men of Springfield were showering her with attention. One of them was Joshua Speed.

Probably because I had pledged myself to Molly, I was relaxed and jovial around Matilda. The others were trying too hard to impress her. While she was not used to such notice, she was cool and detached. As far as she could manage the role, she was not averse to being the occasional coquette. I listened to Speed's gallant worship of her and felt sorry for him.

If I'd allowed myself, I too might have been quite taken with her. To converse with her was a delight. Her brown eyes sparkled with excitement. She surmised that I was unavailable, and we reached a level of familiarity the others could not attain. She loved my stories and anecdotes because they teemed with common life, a world the Springfield luminaries did not know. Because she was tall, it was easier to dance with her. I was more comfortable than I'd been with anyone. With her, I discovered the rhythm of the music, and I moved to it more easily. For the first time, I was enjoying it. I began to wonder whether she was growing a little sweet on me, and the thought was pleasing. Images of Matilda danced through my mind when I should have been focusing on Molly.

Perhaps this was why the doubts began.

At first they flickered into my thoughts when I was drawing up the papers for a case in the office, or when I was walking through the streets of Springfield late in the evening. In the dark of night, they would roll in like the fog that hovered over the silhouettes of the leafless trees, but when I turned the corner and headed back to the town square, the vapor lifted and the crescent moon emerged from behind the large shadow of the newly completed capitol. Which would it be?

I returned to Speed's store and quietly crept into our bed and slept.

But in the morning one thought was the first to emerge and it gnawed at me throughout the day: Could I give Molly the life to which she had become accustomed?

I could not avoid the answer.

Most certainly not.

Many newly wedded couples began their married life in one room at the Globe Tavern.

Could Molly live like that?

Most certainly not.

Although I had a steady income, it was small and not likely to grow larger for some years. When we finally could afford to buy a house, it would be modest. She would have to cook, wash, sew, and clean. Could she live like that?

Most certainly not.

She had grown up in a family with slaves to do the work of the household. She was accustomed to wealth and all its privileges. She was a creature of grace and refinement. Could she be happy with me?

I did not know, but I thought not.

I was right when I told Molly that Speed was the one person who could "counsel and condole" me.

I chose the moment carefully. With the chill of late fall, Speed and I built a late afternoon fire to warm the large room. As we sat by the fireplace, Speed finished tabulating the day's sales, and I read the week's copy of the *Sangamo Journal*.

"Speed, listen to this. It's on the front page under 'Miscellaneous,'" I exclaimed.

He did not look up from his papers and seemed decidedly uninterested.

"It's an article entitled, 'Making Augur Holes with a Gimlet'."

He asked flatly, "Who would ever want to do that?"

"Well, we're about to find out."

I read, "'My boy, what are you doing with that gimlet?' I said the other morning to the flaxen haired urchin, who was laboring with all his might at a piece of board before him. 'Trying to make an augur hole,' was his reply without raising his eye or suspending his operations.

"Precisely the business of at least two-thirds of the world, in this blessed year of our Lord, 1840, is this making of augur holes with a gimlet, I said to myself as I walked musingly onward."

Speed looked up, mildly irritated, "Why are you reading me that foolishness? Their attempts at humor are always miserable."

"It's about to get more interesting," I responded, and then continued reading, "Here is young Mr. A., who has just escaped the merchant's desk...."

Speed's head jerked up. His face showed surprise and interest. "What was that you just read? Read it again."

"Here is young Mr. A., who has just escaped the merchant's desk, or from behind the counter."

"This is starting to sound vaguely familiar," he commented.

"Yes, it's someone who works in a store. I think it's definitely you. Now listen to what comes next. 'Mr. B. is a rabid politician.'"

"Oh, no!" Speed said, "that's you. It must mean the slasher-gaff."

"It certainly sounds like it. Let me read the rest. 'There is a Miss C., who is really a pretty girl....'"

"Who could that be?" he interrupted.

"I don't know," I said, and kept reading, "and who might become a woman a man of sense could be proud of. Now she apes the ton in all things; reads exciting novels, goes to the opera, admires Celeste's dancing, has nearly ceased to blush at the most indecent nudity...."

Speed cried, "What? That's on the front page of the *Sangamo Journal?*"

"Let me continue," I barked at him.

"most indecent nudity, lounges on sofas, glories in her idleness, keeps her bed till noon...."

Speed rose and cried, "Lincoln, someone is making fun of us!"

"It certainly is us, but who is the pretty girl? Whoever could have written this?" I asked.

"Does it say who wrote it?"

"It just says, 'From the Cultivator.'"

"That's a ruse. I'll bet it was Douglas."

"Perhaps, but he publishes anonymously in the *Register*. I'd be surprised if Francis would take something like that from him."

"Francis will tell us who wrote it. We should go see him."

"Yes, tomorrow, but who is Miss C.?" I asked again.

"I'm not sure. Read it again."

I did, but we were both still mystified.

We were getting our supper ready, when he yelled, "It just came to me! It's Matilda!"

"Why, Speed, you are a proper sleuth! That's exactly who it is."

"Those are mean things to say about her."

"Well, as you and I know, no one escapes the merciless cuts of the anonymous pen in this town. What do you suppose Matilda has to do with us?"

"I don't know," he said sheepishly.

As we finished supper, our mood turned more somber.

He began, "Lincoln, you have not seemed yourself these past days. Is something troubling you?"

"Speed, you know me so well."

"What is it?

"Sadly, I cannot share it with you unless I break a pledge of secrecy."

"But, if it is troubling you deeply, sharing it with me could help you live with it."

"Yes, that is so, but I am sworn to keep it between myself and another."

"Perhaps this will help. I have a secret of my own. It also concerns another. I will share it with you, and we will then have the bond of our secrets. No one will know but you and I."

"That is very generous of you, and I will accede to your wishes. What have you kept secret from me?"

"I have proposed to Matilda."

"Why, Speed, what news! Matilda would be a dear and loving wife to you. I wish you all the world she may accept. Did she receive you well?"

"She gave no sign."

"Well, at least she did not refuse you."

"Yes, there is still hope."

He blushed for a moment and then asked me, "Lincoln, what is your secret?"

"Molly and I are engaged to marry."

He seemed momentarily stunned, but his face burst into a broad smile, and he took my hands in his.

"That is indeed a secret, and a capital one at that! We knew you and she were becoming more familiar, but we did not know how familiar. You have made a splendid match. You should be overjoyed, not dismayed."

I looked down at the floor.

"Oh, Speed, if you only knew."

"What troubles you about your good fortune?"

"Oh, I can hardly tell you."

"What is it?"

"I do not think I can give Molly the life she deserves."

"But, Lincoln, she must be the judge of that."

"There is also something more."

"What is it?"

"I too am in love with Matilda."

PART THREE

Chapter Twelve

I Am Utterly Miserable

When I admitted to Speed that I was entranced with Matilda, he could not understand. He said he knew me as a man of my word, and that it was utterly unlike me to have betrayed Molly.

I did not think this was because Matilda had not accepted his proposal. Jealousy was not in Speed's nature. He knew how unusual Matilda was, and how attracted he was to her, and he recognized that I could feel for her as he did. Still, he could not forgive me for deserting Molly for Matilda.

I did my best to explain. Although the letter I had written Eliza Browning was for April Fool's, the truth may have emerged when I doubted whether I would marry. I cloaked it in the jest of who would have me. Perhaps the truth was I did not want to marry. I was attracted to women, but relating to them was something that didn't come easily. I was much more comfortable with men. My thoughts about marrying were hopelessly confused. Molly drew me to her, and gradually I responded. The letters we wrote in the summer brought us closer. When we were together in September and she asked whether I could marry her, I assented. My doubts began the day after. They centered on whether I could give her the life she'd known. But I knew they went deeper. I had loved Annie, and it seemed so simple, but I never felt that way again until I was with Matilda. It was so natural and genuine.

Speed's face was drawn. He turned away and then focused on me intently.

"What you are telling me is that you do not love Molly. Is that true?"

"Yes, I can hardly understand it myself, but it is true."

"Did you ever love her?"

"I believe I did for a while."

"Could you learn to love her again?"

"Perhaps I could, but my doubts are strong."

"There is always the chance that if you marry her, the doubts will ease away."

"But I do not love her enough to try."

Speed hesitated, and thought carefully about what he would say next. He got up from his chair and held the back of it while looking into the fireplace. We had not put a log on the fire while we had been talking. It was down to the coals, although they glowed brightly. He placed another log on the grate, and the flames leaped to devour it.

"Then you will have to tell her," he said quietly without looking at me.

"I have written her a letter. I have it here."

"Will you show it to me?"

I gave him the letter, and he read it carefully.

"Will you deliver it for me?"

"I will not."

"Speed, I have never known you to be an obstinate man. If you will not deliver it, I will get someone else to do it."

"You should burn it."

"Why?"

"Words are passed by or forgotten in private conversation, but once you put your words in writing, they will stand against you. If you have the will and manhood to go and see her, you should speak to her about what you have written in this letter."

"Ah, you who are not the lawyer advise me sensibly."

"You are not yourself."

"How soon should I see her?"

"As soon as you can."

I could not bring myself to do it. It would have been so much easier to write a letter, but Speed was right. I had to go to her and tell her the truth.

For the next few days, I slept fitfully. When I woke in the night, I could not return to sleep. I imagined Molly's face as I asked her to release me. It haunted me throughout the night.

Preferable to restless misery was walking through the isolated streets of Springfield. Sometimes a dog would bark or a hog might grunt in its sleep. The outlines of the stores and houses were recognizable in the darkness. When it rained, I buttoned my shirt collar around my neck; when the wind tore at me, I bundled tighter in my coat; and when snow drifted lightly over me, I brushed it from my hair.

And as I walked on Washington Street approaching the town square with the half moon just above the cupola of the Capitol, in the mist ahead of me, I spied a distinct shape—the form of an old woman. When I came closer, I could see she had white hair and was dressed in black. Was it the same one I had seen before? She fixed her eyes on mine, as if in a moment of recognition, and then turned into the alley. I called to her, but she disappeared into the mist and shadows.

As I moved on, my thoughts were jumbled images from my life before and projections of my life to come. Both were bleak and unforgiving. In struggling with this,

I found my mind doing something unusual. Somehow I removed myself from myself as if looking at myself. It was oddly comforting.

One night, when I was in this trancelike state, I nearly stumbled over a slumped bundle of rags on the bottom step of the new state capitol.

Curious, I kicked at the odd heap.

An audible groan caused me to jump back in fright. Gradually unfolding itself was an unmistakable human form. Greasy, matted, black hair hung down over a pallid, hollow face. A grizzled gray-white beard revealed it was a man. In the dim light from the lamppost, I could see in his eyes an appeal for help. Though I was repulsed, I did not shy away.

I peered down at him.

As he looked up, it seemed as if he was trying to place me in a world far removed.

He could hardly speak. All he uttered was a scratchy, "Aaaaabe?"

I was as perplexed as he.

"Who are you?" I asked.

Now came a broken croak, "Nelllssso... ...lllyyy."

It was a mystery I could not solve. I was about to abandon hope when a glimpse of his face brought me back to a former time.

"Nelson Alley? Are you Nelson Alley?" I cried.

"Yes... Abe..." he bent his face down covering his knees.

"Nelson," I cried again, "Whatever could have happened to you? What are you doing here? Let me help you."

He could say nothing more. Fortunately we were close to Speed's store, and even though we would have to endure the stench, I knew Speed would offer shelter to someone without a home.

"Nelson, I will help you walk to where I live. It is nearby. You must try to stand. Take my arm."

He was very weak, but I was able to lift him from the step, and ever so slowly, we crossed the street to Speed's store. We negotiated the steps up to the door, and then I led him through to my haven of warmth and shelter. Nelson collapsed on the floor and fell asleep immediately.

When we awoke the next morning, I told Speed about Nelson. He had been one of my most treasured friends from New Salem. He bought the tavern from James Rutledge when the Rutledge family moved north to their farm near Petersburg. Nelson hired Henry Onstot to manage it. I lived at the tavern for three years, and because I had little money, Nelson reduced my rent. During one dry spell, I couldn't pay him anything, and he allowed it was fine with him if I stayed on anyway. I was deeply grateful.

Later in the morning, Nelson was strong enough to tell us the story of his misfortune. As New Salem was dying, he tried to keep the tavern open. Gradually, the proceeds dried up. Nelson realized New Salem could not survive, and he moved to Springfield with what little money he had left. When that ran out, he was at the mercy of the world. He had no family to care for him. He had been living as a beggar for the past few months, and winter was coming.

When Nelson finished, I told him I would find him a place to live and to start over. Speed agreed that he should stay until I made the arrangements. It was the least I could do for someone who had once been so helpful to me.

Helping someone whose plight was worse than mine caused my turmoil to ease—but not for long. I was still reluctant to visit Molly. I knew it would be dishonorable to ask her to release me from our engagement, but I was certain I did not love her as I should. I could not live with my doubts, nor could I live with what they would cause me to do.

Finally I could see only one way out. I wrote Molly asking to see her. Her note in return conveyed surprise at the formality of my request, but she chose the next afternoon for us to visit together in the parlor at the Edwards' house.

The walk from Speed's store to the Edwards' house was short, but it was like a march to the gallows. I looked at the ground, my heart raced, my hands were sweaty, and I breathed deeply. Fortunately, the streets were empty.

When I arrived and knocked on the door, Elizabeth Edwards greeted me and led me to the parlor. There, sitting on the horsehair couch where we first courted, was Molly. She wore a dark blue dress with a white pattern across the top. Holding her hands together, she looked up at me demurely.

I sat down awkwardly beside her.

"Mr. Lincoln," she said tensely, "I am surprised you have come calling as if we barely knew each other. I hear you have not been well. I hope that is the cause of your distraction."

"It is true. I have not been myself these past few days."

"I wish you a quick recovery and a return to genial spirits. It is not like you to be out of sorts for long."

"No, I would prefer it were not so."

"I hope it is nothing more than a passing ailment. This is the time of year for such things. They can afflict any of us. If it were more than that, I am sure Dr. Henry would see you."

"I'm afraid it's beyond his ability to help."

"Whatever can have caused you to be so perturbed?"

"I cannot sleep. I do not want to eat. I am not proper company for any man or woman."

"What ever can it be?"

I looked at the ground. I looked at the portraits above the fireplace. I could not look at her.

Finally, I said, "I must ask you to release me from our engagement."

She gave a startled cry, sighed heavily, put her hands over her face and began to weep.

The tears continued, but gradually she collected herself.

"Why?… Why this sudden change of heart?"

I could hardly reply, but the words began to stumble out. "Oh, if you only knew what agony this has been. It is no fault of yours."

"Then what has caused you to think differently of me?"

"I cannot give you the life you deserve. You were raised in a wealthy family. Your father is one of Kentucky's leading men. If we are married, you will live in a room at the Globe Tavern until we can afford a modest house. You will have to do the household chores yourself."

"My sister Frances and William Wallace began their marriage in a room at the Globe."

"But William is a doctor and will be a man of means. Elizabeth married Ninian, and he is the son of the former governor. She already lives in a house that must rival yours in Lexington. Can you live a simple life in Springfield when they are so well-fixed?"

"But that is for me to decide, not you."

"You fancy what our life would be, but as it unfolded, you would resent the choice you made."

"Do you not think I have weighed this? I have, and I do not find you wanting. There must be more to it."

"I do not love you as I should."

"But what has caused this change? Just a few weeks ago, you pledged your love. What has caused you to withdraw it?"

"I cannot say."

"Is it Elizabeth? It must be Elizabeth who has put this in your head. She has turned against us and counseled me not to marry you because our backgrounds are so different and because we are such different people. She must have spoken with you."

"No," I replied,

"Mr. Lincoln, you are not yourself. You are the most honest man I know. You cannot withhold this from me!"

I said nothing.

"What is this? It must be someone else! Someone has crept past your feelings for me and stolen the key to your heart. Whoever can it be?"

I looked ahead at the fireplace and said nothing. I could feel her glare, and then I heard her wounded cry.

"Matilda! It's Matilda. It's the traitor who has shared my room and my confidence!"

I nodded.

"Woe is me. The deceiver shall be deceived!"

I did not know what this meant, but it caused her to weep again uncontrollably.

She leaned toward me.

I drew her down on my knee and kissed her.

Through her sobs, she spoke haltingly.

"Mr. Lincoln... if you desire it... I will release you... but I have not changed my mind...and feel as always... and I will hold the question an open one."

We then parted, and I walked out through the receiving room, the entryway, and the front door.

As I walked home, I felt a total emptiness.

An image flashed into my thoughts. I was back in our Indiana cabin taking aim at the wild turkey with Papa's musket. I could see it through the crack in the logs. I fired, destroying its head. Blood spurted into the trees and all over the ground.

It was followed by an image of what I had just done to Molly.

Again, I had a gun in my hands. I raised it and took aim at a great white bird. I pulled the trigger and felt the blast jerk into my shoulder. Red erupted from the bird's crushed chest and gushed over its broken wing. The poor creature struggled as it plunged down toward the brown prairie grass. I left it to suffer and die.

When I returned to Speed's store, he was not there. I climbed the ladder to the upstairs loft and sat down on our bed. I rolled over and fell into a deep, troubled sleep.

In the late afternoon I awoke and climbed back down the ladder. Speed was at the far end of the store by the fireplace. The fire, which he had just lit, was beginning to crackle. He was reading the week's copy of the *Sangamo Journal*.

He turned toward me and called, "Here is friend Lincoln raised from the dead."

I walked unsteadily to my chair and did not respond to his lighthearted greeting.

When I sat down and stretched my legs toward the fire, he looked over at me with deep concern.

I looked away from him.

He asked, "Lincoln, did you speak with her?"

I did not reply.

He sat quietly and looked into the fire.

Ending the silence, he spoke again, "How did she respond?"

"She loves me, and I have caused her to suffer."

"You will suffer for that."

"Yes, I do not know how I will live with myself."

"You will learn."

"I am glad of that."

"How did you leave it with her?"

"I drew her down my knee and kissed her."

Speed paused for a moment, reflected, and then said, "This last thing is a bad mistake, but it cannot now be helped. You must promise not to see her."

"I will not see her."

Speed rose and stood by the fireplace. When he looked at me, his face was pained.

"Is there something else?" I asked.

"Separately all these matters cause us grief, but now they have conjoined."

"What is it?"

"You know I wrote my mother in the fall about returning to Kentucky."

"I never gave it any credence."

"She has written to say she would welcome me."

"But why would you return?"

"When my father died, my mother thought she could manage our family's affairs. She has written that it would be helpful if I returned. I do not wish to manage this store much longer. I will sell my share to Hurst and leave for Farmington in the spring.

"But you have many friends here in Springfield who would offer you a position."

"My prospects here in Springfield have dimmed."

"Yes, the economy has faded, but your own prospects remain bright."

"They do not."

"You are concealing something. This is not like you, unless it is… Matilda!"

He was silent.

"Has Matilda refused you?"

"She has," he replied.

"Oh, Speed, we are both forsaken—and I am to lose my best friend and my prospects for marriage on the same day. I am utterly miserable."

Chapter Thirteen

To Mask My Sadness in Mirth

For me, January 1, 1841 ushered in a year that promised to be as bleak as the winter weather that gripped Springfield. Frigid air crawled in through the cracks in Speed's store. A raging fire heated only a small section of the first floor—not the upstairs where we slept. We hardly saw the sun. Day after day of gray sky hung above the leafless trees. There were no colors in the world but gray, brown, and black, and occasionally the white of the snow. It was colder than anyone could remember.

In November, I was elected to my fourth term in the legislature.

In a special session that began on December 7, 1840, we wrestled with the financial issues that were stalking the state. An interest payment of $175,000 was due on January 1 for the bonds that financed the state's internal improvements. The Whigs narrowly defeated the Democrats' proposal to kill the state bank. The economic crisis ended the Whig dreams for an Illinois where the market economy could create opportunity for all.

I decided I would not run again in 1842. I had learned as much as I could in the legislature. I would never hold a seat just for the sake of occupying it.

With the prospect of Stuart serving another term in Congress, it was time for us to dissolve the partnership of Stuart and Lincoln. Because Stuart was not present to teach me, I was not learning the subtleties of the law. There was so much more to it than writing declarations and helping people collect debts. When and how would I learn it?

In late 1840, I began to listen more carefully to the informal conversations among friends that might apprise me of an opportunity. I was uncertain when this might come.

Speed's decision to return to Kentucky was an unwanted surprise. Since his father's death, he knew it was a possibility, but I did not think he would leave Springfield. I could not imagine my life without him, but at least he would not leave until the spring. I had an open invitation to visit him and his family at Farmington, their plantation near Louisville.

Willam Butler, with whom I had served in the Black Hawk War and in the legislature, invited me to live with him and his family after Speed's departure. His wife had already provided me with some of my meals and mended my clothes. It was a suitable arrangement, but it was one more change.

And then there was the matter of Molly. Speed was right. I would not see her, even though she held the question open. If only she had rejected me and declared an end to our affair. I caused her to suffer. And what was her offense? Simply to love me. She was above reproach, but because I was not true to my word, I betrayed my honor and sullied my reputation.

In the first week in January, all this crashed down on me.

When I was in New Salem and Annie died, I retreated into myself. There, in that dark place, I had remained for several weeks.

This was different, and it was worse. Neither Annie nor I caused our misfortune. It was what fate decreed. Neither of us could struggle against it. We were at the mercy of what would be.

This was different. I caused it to happen. I caused Molly's suffering. On a sunny, fall afternoon by the Sangamon River, I succumbed to an impulse. I did not subject it to cold, calculating, unimpassioned reason. The next day I regretted it. Could I ever make a decision like this again? Could I ever give anyone my word? Could I ever trust myself again?

I did not think so. There was no way out.

The black despair oozed in and stayed. Before, when it came, it might stay briefly or a little longer, but eventually it lifted.

I forced myself to rise in the morning. I staggered across the street, sat in the back of the house chamber in the statehouse, cast one or two votes, and then left. I crawled back into bed.

When I was not asleep, I stared at the rough brown boards which served as walls, the darkened rafters that supported the roof, or the two dormers with windows that admitted minimal light. It was dark and uninviting during the day. If I felt so inclined, I lumbered out of bed, placed a rickety chair in the dormer, and looked vacantly out the window. The Capitol, which reminded me of my unmet responsibilities, loomed nearby in the gray gloom of the January day.

For a few days, I awoke, dressed, climbed down the ladder, and walked to the statehouse to listen to the debate and then to vote, but gradually I lost interest in doing that. My colleagues were perplexed as I had rarely missed a vote in my three terms as a legislator. I spoke to no one, and no one spoke to me.

I had no interest in food. Speed prepared dinner

or supper for me, but I refused his overtures. My only nourishment was an occasional cup of water.

I saw that Speed had removed my razor and all the knives from their familiar places.

I could not control my thoughts. I had not the will. Unbidden images rose, afflicted me, and faded—Speed leaving for Kentucky, John Todd Stuart removing the sign "Stuart and Lincoln" from his office door, the legislators voting down internal improvements, and Douglas humiliating me in debate.

There was one which remained longer than the others and took longer to fade. Even if I tried to concentrate on something happier, it returned. It was Molly weeping when I told her I no longer loved her.

At other times, the images, which I had worn threadbare in my earlier despair, arose once more: my gaunt mother, the little boy she bore who died four days later, my kind sister dying in childbirth, and Annie's lovely face.

The spiral of these recurring thoughts took me further and further down. It was as if I were at the bottom of a well. There was no way to climb up. I was condemned to lie there and die.

For a week, I remained in our bed. Though Speed slept next to me and tried to free me from the grip of my despair, I did not acknowledge him. I lay in the dingy, semi-darkness of the day and the full darkness of the night.

I was incapable of representing the people of my district.

I was unable to respond to the kindness of a friend.

I was lost inside myself.

Speed could bear it no longer.

He climbed up the ladder, walked to the dormer, and pulled the rickety chair to the side of the bed where I lay. I was awake and saw him sit down in the chair, He looked distraught.

He said firmly, "Lincoln, you must rally or you will die."

I looked at him but said nothing.

He raised his voice, "You must speak to me."

It took what little energy I had left, but I leaned up and responded hoarsely, "I am now the most miserable man living…. If what I feel were equally distributed to the whole human family… there would not be one cheerful face on the earth…. Whether I shall ever be better I cannot tell…. I awfully forebode not…. To remain as I am is impossible…. I must die or be better."

The effort of saying this caused me to fall back on the bed.

"You must see Dr. Henry. He is deeply concerned for you."

I said nothing.

"Your friends are worried you may take your own life."

I had to respond to this.

"That is what Bowling Green told me when I stayed with him after Annie died. I will tell you what I told him. 'I am not afraid of death, but I have an irrepressible desire to live till I can be assured that the world is a little better for my having lived in it.'"

Speed persuaded me to see Dr. Henry, who was five years older than I. He came to Springfield in 1833 from New York via Cincinnati where he studied medicine. He was a political colleague and a personal friend.

For six days, I walked to his office and spent half the day with him. His diagnosis was that I was suffering from hypochondriasis—a debilitating melancholia that could be treated.

Once he made the diagnosis, Dr. Henry began the treatments. First he bled me to begin clearing out the black bile which he believed was causing my illness. He cut me with a razor to draw the blood. A large amount spilled out. Next came the blistering in which hot glass cups were placed on my temples. This pulled the blood up toward my skin, and he attached leeches to suck out more blood. After this, I had to ingest compounds that caused vomiting and diarrhea. Following that, I fasted for three days. Then I took a variety of stimulants: coffee, black pepper, garlic, mustard, and quinine. He gave me mercury to continue the purging, and which, after a few days, turned my stools green. Dr. Henry was cheered by this because it meant the black bile had been removed. Finally, I took warm baths to make me sweat, followed immediately by cold baths.

I am not sure if it was a result of the treatments, but gradually I reacquired a level of energy that allowed me to return to my life. While the black despair eased a bit, and the images of sorrow and suffering no longer paraded through my thoughts, my spirits still sagged.

I was able to return to the legislature, but I was not myself. Some of my friends were honest and told me I was much thinner, if not emaciated. My Whig colleagues said they had missed me, and they attributed the passage of a controversial piece of legislation to my absence. The Democratic scheme to pack the

Illinois Supreme Court with five new justices was approved in the house by a vote of 45–43. As a result, Douglas would be appointed to the court and continue to outpace me in his quest for political advancement.

There was resolution to one important matter in my life. I learned that Stephen Logan had decided to replace my friend Baker with a new partner. Logan knew that Stuart and I were ending our partnership, and he approached me to ask my level of interest in joining him. Stuart urged me to accept because he regarded Logan as the finest lawyer in Sangamon County. I knew Logan would be an excellent mentor. Stuart taught me to immerse into specific cases, but what I had not gained was a deeper knowledge of the law. Logan told me that if I worked with him, I would broaden myself as a lawyer.

As Stuart and I dissolved our partnership, we reviewed our unresolved cases.

In *Cannan v. Kenney*, the case of the stolen horse, on July 14, 1838, Cannan withdrew his suit. However, on May 10, 1839, he asked us to file a second lawsuit. Logan and Baker represented the defendant Kenney. On July 16, 1839, the case was tried, but Logan proposed a motion of nonsuit. This was sustained, and based on insufficient evidence, the jury did not deliver a verdict. In addition, the court ordered the plaintiff Cannan to pay the defendant Kenney's costs in the suit. Cannan could continue to pursue his case, which he did. On August 19, 1839, I filed an appeal on behalf of Cannan to the Illinois Supreme Court. The case was in continuance when Stuart and I reviewed it. In all likelihood, the Supreme Court would hear it in July. I agreed to represent Cannan at the appeal.

Another unresolved case was our lawsuit against General Adams on behalf of the Anderson family. The suit involved the land that the Andersons believed General Adams had stolen from them. This suit was still being delayed, and I agreed to pursue it. In the interim, we learned that General Adams had been indicted in New York for a similar offense. Rather than facing trial, he had abandoned his family and fled the state.

For the rest of the winter and into the early spring, Speed was preparing to leave Springfield and return to Kentucky. Ever so slowly, I began to accommodate myself to the idea of life without him nearby.

In early April, he proposed that we celebrate our friendship with a special occasion. One afternoon he returned to the store with palpable excitement.

He cried, "Lincoln, there's news!"

Under his arm he was carrying a copy of the week's *Journal*. He unfolded it on the counter and pointed to a picture of an elephant.

"Here it is. Seely's circus is coming to town! It will cheer you up immeasurably."

"Wonderful!" I cried. "I love the circus. I saw my first one when I lived in New Salem. I borrowed a horse and rode to Springfield to see it."

Speed asked, "Should we invite someone to join us?"

"Of course, who should it be?"

"I have an idea. It's someone of whom you will approve."

"Who could it be?"

"I will ask Ninian and Elizabeth if we can take Julia."

Julia was their four-year old daughter, and a sprightlier young lady one never could find.

"Agreed," I said, "but you will have to be the one who asks Elizabeth."

"I will go this moment. It will cost us each fifty cents, but it's half price for Julia."

Two days later, Speed and I walked to the noontime parade of the circus performers and animals. Blonde-haired Julia skipped along beside us. The tent was on the lawn by the east side of the Capitol, and the parade route was three trips around the town square. When the parade ended, the animals and the performers would enter the tent, followed by the patrons.

As we arrived, there was a huge crowd around the square. They parted for Julia to come to the front and allowed us to accompany her. The brass band played a march followed by a waltz and repeated the pattern. As the time crept toward noon, expectations ran high.

With a fanfare from the band, the showman led the performers through the crowd onto Sixth Street. Behind the showman came the high wire artists dressed in red and blue, tight-fitting costumes and carrying their balance poles; the female dancers in their frilly Parisian dresses and the males in country dress-ups; the equestrians, one of whom was the lilliputian master Johnson, seven years old; the sword swallower and the fire eater; an assortment of pirates, vagabonds, and gypsies; and finally the clowns in their multicolored, baggy outfits with their faces painted white with huge red, upturned mouths. The clowns worked the crowd, and little Julia cooed with glee as one of them held her up and showed her off to the multitude.

When the showman and the performers bid their adieus, a row of cages, each pulled by horses, rolled down Sixth Street. The first one aroused a cheer, and those ensuing were welcomed with "oohs and aahs" or audible gasps. As the horses strained to tug the first large, barred crate past us, we spotted a royal Bengal tiger pacing furiously as he eyed the crowd. Next came the black-and-white striped zebra, which caused Julia to cheer and clap her hands. Then came a monstrous gorilla looking quite bored; perhaps he would have preferred to read the newspaper. In the last cage, was a gentle hippopotamus with its massive body, huge head, and short, stumpy legs.

The crowd cheered as the last cage rolled past, but it did not realize a greater treat was yet to come.

They gave way and parted for safety as the behemoth of the jungle, a giant pachyderm lumbered down the streets of the town square with a turbaned rider behind his ears atop his neck, and two couples, the gentlemen in evening clothes and the women in ballroom gowns, sitting in a large basket on his back. Never had we seen such a thing on the streets of our town. I took little Julia in my arms as she trembled with fear and wonder. We caught our breath knowing the elephant would return twice more and then vanish into memory.

The band played another fanfare, and we joined the group entering the tent. Thanks to Speed's quick response to the advertisement in the Journal, we had seats in the front row.

The circus itself was a kaleidoscope of sounds, smells, and sights. Popular tunes blared out from a calliope, the air smelled of sawdust and animal dung, and the showman introduced each act. In between the performances, three jugglers tossed bowling pins in the air, and the clowns visited with the crowd.

There were two acts that thrilled the crowd, and they were Julia's favorites as well.

A pretty young woman trotted out in the ring on a gallant racehorse. Faster and faster, the horse galloped while the young woman showed off her skill. Horse and rider blended together in a graceful flow. At the climax of her performance, she stood up on the horse's back and balanced on one foot while raising her back leg so that it paralleled the ground. Her white dress undulated in the breeze, and a streamer billowed from her hands. She eased back down onto the horse to thunderous applause.

Shortly thereafter, the showman disappeared and then reemerged with an enormous snake wrapped around him. I feared that Julia would turn away in tears and ask to go home, but I was mistaken. She was fascinated with the creature and looked at it with utter delight. The showman told us it was an anaconda from South America and that it crushed its prey to death. I had never seen anything so frightful. It swayed its head out toward us while rapidly thrusting its six-inch, forked tongue into the air. When the showman moved toward the crowd, people turned away in horror. Only Julia was brave enough to look at the snake. When she reached to touch it, the crowd gasped.

When the circus was over, Speed and I walked an ebullient Julia back to the Edwards' house on Aristocracy Hill. She hugged us both and rushed inside to tell her parents about her adventure.

Speed and I talked on our way home.

"That certainly dispelled your gloom," began Speed.

"Yes, I can't thank you enough. You were right to think of it as a way to celebrate our friendship. I will always remember this day."

"What will you remember from it?"

"I will remember my kind friend who helped lift my spirits. I will remember the exotic wonders of the circus. I will remember Julia sitting between us rapt with wonder and delight."

"Will you remember anything else?"

"Yes, Speed, I will remember the clowns. For some reason, most people are repelled by the clowns, but I am fascinated by them. Their jokes are as bad, if not worse, than mine. Their suits are baggy and colorful and evoke laughter. I am told that clowns are often sad people masking their gloom in mirth. That is my task—to mask my sadness in mirth."

Chapter Fourteen

It Would Just Kill Me to Marry Her

In April, Speed returned to Kentucky, and I moved to Butler's house to live with him and his family. I was faithful to my promise not to see Molly.

Over the next few months, the deep melancholy abated, but much of the joy I had known in my life was gone. The evening gatherings of friends around the fireplace at Speed's store were a distant reminder of a former life.

I had no choice but to trudge onward.

After I stumbled across him on the steps of the statehouse, Nelson Alley lived with us for a few days. We found him a room on the outskirts of town, and Speed and I paid his landlord three months' rent. We also shared his living expenses to help him get started.

When Speed left, I visited Nelson each week. It was heartening to learn that he'd found work at one of the inns south of the town square. Boarding was part of his pay, and he could afford his rent.

Speed told me he lived with melancholy by trying to help others. This was good advice. Helping Nelson gave him hope and lifted my spirits.

Walking home from one of my visits to Nelson, I came across two little girls who were sitting on a large trunk and crying profusely.

"Whatever is the matter?" I asked them.

At first, they could not reply through their tears. Finally, between the two of them, I was able to learn what had happened.

"Mother and Father have left us…." heaved the first through her sobs.

"It's our vacation…." sniffled the second.

"And we are going away…." continued the first.

"But where are your parents?" I asked.

"At the depot," cried both at once.

"What are they doing there?"

The first one ceased her weeping and finished the story. "They are waiting for us… and the dray hasn't come… and our trunk is here… and we are left behind…."

"Now, girls," I said, "I can help."

I picked up the trunk, carried it on my shoulders, and bade them follow me. We walked together, two little ducklings and a laden giraffe, and their spirits rose immeasurably.

It was only three blocks to the depot. They rushed to their parents, who thanked me extravagantly for my simple good deed, and all was well.

When I settled in at Butler's, I began to notice Mrs. Butler's sister, Sarah Rickard. Sarah had been 12 when I first visited with her aunt and uncle in 1837. It was now four years later, and she had bloomed considerably.

When Sarah was a girl, we enjoyed telling stories to each other, and I took her to some of the children's entertainments in Springfield. When she became a young woman, we attended some of the theatrical productions.

One day in May, I opened Butler's Bible and read her the story of Abraham and Sarah.

"Sarah," I said to her playfully, "You will become Abraham's wife."

"Oh no, Mr. Lincoln," she replied, "I am too young to be thinking of matrimony, and you will always be an older brother to me."

I wondered, if perhaps, I'd meant it more seriously than I supposed.

On July 8, I appeared before the Illinois Supreme Court representing Manly Cannan for whom we were appealing the decision of the Circuit Court of Sangamon County to sustain the motion of nonsuit in his suit against Matthew Kenney. The decision of nonsuit meant the jury had been absolved from reaching a verdict.

The reason the nonsuit was accepted was that Cannan's horse was not in his direct possession when Kenney took it. In preparing for the appeal, I wrote a Bill of Exceptions. There I detailed the confusing history of what happened to the horse. In the fall of 1836, Cannan lent it to John Harris who rode it home to Sangamon County. John Harris gave the horse to his brother James Harris with payment for feeding and safekeeping through the winter. He did not tell him who owned the horse. When James Harris found his horse feed running low, he gave the horse to his brother Robert who had sufficient feed for the winter. When the grass rose in the spring, Robert Harris turned the horse out on the prairie with his own horses. While the horse was running loose, Kenney seized it and refused to give it back to Cannan when he returned to Sangamon County in the fall of 1837.

My appeal was based on two arguments: that the judgment should have been rendered for the plaintiff, Cannan, and that the court erred in instructing the jury as in the case of a nonsuit.

I had prepared carefully for the appeal, but I was slightly nervous as I walked into the Capitol and entered the Supreme Court chamber. It was plush compared to the other courtrooms I'd known, and ceremonial in appearance. The judges, including Stephen A. Douglas, sat on a semicircular platform at the front. It was bordered by an elegant, red oak railing. Behind the judges hung an imposing red curtain. In front of it sat Samuel Treat, the chief judge. In the middle of the room were two tables covered with green cloths for the lawyers representing the opposing sides. A metal chandelier attached itself to the ceiling like an enormous spider.

For an inexperienced lawyer like me, the chamber was intimidating. I was used to plain courtrooms and not the ornate setting of the Supreme Court.

Adding to the intensity of the occasion was that the attorney representing Matthew Kenney was my new partner, Stephen Logan, who had been retained prior to our partnership.

Nonetheless, as I began to speak, my preparation gave me confidence—that and the merits of the case I was arguing. The proceedings lasted under an hour, and as we were dismissed, we were informed that the court would announce its ruling the following morning.

After a sleepless night, I sat at my table in the Supreme Court chamber to hear the ruling entitled "Opinion of the Court." It was read by Justice Sidney Breece who had written it.

"Cannan brought his action of trespass," he began, "in the Circuit Court of Sangamon against Kenney for seizing a horse and converting it to his own use. The defendant pleaded not guilty."

Justice Breece reviewed the process whereby the horse was owned by Cannan, transferred to the Harris brothers, and seized by Kenney.

He continued, "The defendant then moved the Court to instruct the jury as in a case of nonsuit, on the ground that there was no evidence that the defendant took the horse from the possession of the plaintiff. Which motion the Court sustained; to which the plaintiff excepted, and judgment being entered against him for the costs, he has brought his case here by writ of errors, and assigns for errors this direction of the Court."

After enumerating the reasons for the Supreme Court's decision, Justice Breece read the decision itself.

"We are of the opinion, that the facts in this case abundantly show, a sufficient possession on the part of the plaintiff to entitle him to this action against the defendant, a mere wrong-doer and a stranger. The judgment of the Circuit Court directing the nonsuit is accordingly reversed with costs, and the cause remanded to the Circuit Court of Sangamon County with instructions to award a venire de novo."

Because there was little likelihood of a new trial, the *venire de novo*, I had won the appeal, and Cannan would recover his horse plus costs. Logan shook my hand and added in a whisper, "Well done."

A few days later, when I reflected on the case of *Cannan v. Kenney*, I was inclined to think that four years was too long to return a horse to its rightful owner. But as I reflected further, I realized that the steps were in place to ensure a deliberate and fair result. What I learned from all my books had transpired. It was hardly a perfect process, but it was a thorough one. It did take an appeal to resolve the case, and the Supreme Court did not hear every appeal, but it found merit in ours and ultimately ruled in our favor. While there were errors,

there was also redress of those errors. I was proud to
be part of a system that was grounded in our American
democratic ideals and English traditions.

While I was gratified by the outcome of *Cannan v.
Kenney* and although my melancholy had lifted, I was still
in the grip of a lassitude I could not overcome. Before
the legislature adjourned in March, I reestablished my
presence there. Logan and I began our partnership in
April, and I was already learning procedural nuances.
But life still felt dismal, hollow, and flat.

Perhaps it was associated with the departure of
Speed, but I couldn't avoid the probability that it had
to do with Molly. From my friends, I learned that she
hoped I would return to the social activities in Springfield. The image of her distress at our parting continued to haunt me. Couldn't she accept that we were not
suited for each other? I told Butler's wife that it would
just kill me to marry her.

And yet, I had broken my promise to her. She loved
me, and I rejected her. How could I avoid my responsibility for her suffering? It was a dilemma from which I
could not escape.

In June, I received a letter from Speed in which he
urged me to visit him and his family at Farmington,
the plantation near Louisville. When I proposed this to
Logan, he agreed to an absence of six weeks, excluding
the time for travel. The best route, which took a week,
was carriage to St. Louis and steamboat to Louisville.
My plan was to stay with Speed during August and
early September.

The weather on the carriage ride was unbearably
hot. I boarded the boat, and we journeyed south to

the Ohio River. The Mississippi was a steam bath. Not until we began to paddle east on the Ohio did the heat subside.

As the steamboat powered up the Ohio, from the deck railing, I looked out at the northern bank. Because we were nearing Rockport and Anderson's Creek, close to my Indiana home, the shore was growing familiar.

When I had set out for New Orleans with Allen Gentry 12 years earlier, the world was opening to me. I embraced it and was eager to learn and grow. Upon my return to the scenes of my youth, I felt only confusion and sadness. As the steamboat paddle churned the water day and night, slowly and deliberately, moving the boat forward, I could see no purpose in life but to plod ahead doing little more than keeping myself alive. Images of death came to mind. Here was where my mother died of the milk sick, where my sister died in childbirth, and my infant brother died after living four days. How could I look out upon this with anything other than bitterness and grief?

When I arrived in Louisville, Speed was there at the dock. He greeted me effusively, and we enjoyed a pleasant journey to Farmington atop his horse-drawn cart. Just being with him again lifted my spirits.

Although he had described Farmington to me before, I was not expecting its grandeur. How typical of Speed to be so understated and humble. My first impression was astonishment that one family could own such a huge tract of land. I could see the main house from the distance as we rode closer. It was an elegant brick structure highlighted with light green shutters and a four pillared, white portico above the front door. White railing bordered the portico and swept down the front stairs to welcome visitors. Three large brick chimneys announced warm, glowing fires in the colder months.

As we drove up to the front of the house, Speed's mother, three sisters, and brother were gathered on the portico to meet me. They were a jolly group, and their welcome was an auspicious beginning.

My day at Farmington began with a horse ride through the different contours of the plantation. One day it was into the woods, and the next it was through the fields. The family offered me a horse for the duration of my visit, and I rode it constantly. Prior to my visit to Farmington, I thought horses were functional and my horsemanship passable. But there I saw my horse as a creature of beauty and grace, and in my early morning rides, I felt my body adapting to the motion of the animal and flowing with the horse's distinct gaits. I learned to give myself up to the will of an animal I could trust.

I rarely ate breakfast, but at Farmington it was an important meal. The family gathered to discuss the day's activities. Eventually my day settled into a pattern, but there was a wide variety of choices. After breakfast, on most days, there were morning walks. The variation was the group that spontaneously assembled and the destination chosen.

Sometimes Speed and I were joined by his sisters, sometimes by his mother, and sometimes we walked by ourselves. All were delightful excursions on which the conversation was alternately serious and lighthearted. If politics arose, the discussion was never heated because we were all Whigs. When we were alone, Speed inquired about the affairs of our friends in Springfield, but his interest in Molly diminished when he learned I had not seen her since December.

After the morning walk, we gathered around the dining room table once more for a hearty dinner. I sat next to a different family member at each of the meals. Only Speed and his mother had permanent seats, at the head and foot of the table.

Each afternoon, I rode my horse into the city of Louisville to visit with James Speed at his office. Speed's brother was a lawyer, and we had much in common. He had shelves of books in his office on many subjects, and I borrowed from them frequently. We enjoyed many leisurely conversations on a variety of topics. He was interested in my political views and my hopes for a future in politics.

James Speed was the only person I spoke to about slavery. While he was troubled by the nature of it, he asked me to consider the 50 slaves at Farmington. His family did its best to give them tolerable lives. The slaves were content, and treating them benignly was not only humane, but it also made sense financially.

While I continued to see slavery as an injustice, I did not argue the point with him. I was, after all, a guest, and I did have to grant him his argument that the slaves at Farmington were well cared for and seemed happy.

One afternoon I rode into the city for treatment of a painful tooth. The doctor decided against extracting it, but the remedy, a vile tasting ointment, was only partially successful.

The highlight of the day for the entire family was supper. The meal was prepared and served by the house slaves. It varied from mutton, pork, and fish for the main course, served with vegetables grown on the plantation. Our favorite dessert was peaches and cream. The peaches came from the orchard near the vegetable garden.

While the meal was always delicious, the table conversation was the meal's delight. It lasted well into the evening and covered all subjects from politics and religion to observations on the latest books everyone was reading. Interspersed was repartee and banter. I particularly enjoyed sitting next to Speed's sister Mary. We were relaxed and occasionally flippant with each other. I chided her that I would have to shut her in her room to prevent her from committing assault and battery on me.

One night at supper I committed a faux pas. When the mutton was served, I found a small bowl of mint jelly in front of my place. As I'd never encountered jelly with dinner, I was flummoxed and emptied the contents onto my plate. One of the slaves noticed and brought out more mint jelly. When I saw the others taking small amounts for their plates, I apologized and said, "I seem to have taken more than my share." Fortunately the response was hearty laughter.

Early in my visit, Speed said he had a surprise he would reveal for us at dinner. That afternoon, as I wandered through the dining room, I noticed that the table was set for one more. Could Speed be bringing a guest?

Before supper, the family gathered in one of the parlors. The slave, who had been assigned to me during my time at Farmington, took special care dressing me for the evening. When I entered the parlor, I did, in fact, get a surprise. Standing next to Speed and doting on him, stood a lovely young woman with dark hair, black eyes, a pretty face, and a trim figure. Her name was Fanny Henning, and she lived on the plantation next to the Speed family. Oddly, Speed had met her only recently. He seemed quite taken by her. When the evening concluded, Mary said to me, "Have you ever seen a sweeter girl?"

Fanny joined Speed and me on our walks and we were a jolly threesome. At the end of August, Speed told me he was going to propose to Fanny, and he enlisted my aid. I was not surprised. In affairs of the heart, Speed moved quickly. He had proposed to Matlilda whom he barely knew. Fanny was ideal for Speed, and I could wish him nothing but success in winning her affection.

Fanny lived with her guardian, Uncle Jeremiah, and my task was to occupy him with conversation while Speed met with Fanny to propose to her. He was apparently deeply interested in politics, so my mission was not a difficult one.

The plot worked perfectly. Uncle Jeremiah was charming, and he was well versed in Whig politics. The glowing couple returned to the parlor where we were chatting amiably. Speed asked him for Fanny's hand. Uncle Jeremiah was momentarily stunned, but he recovered quickly, took Speed's hands, and said, "My dear boy, nothing could please me more!" I was thrilled for my friend, but it did highlight his success and my failure.

In early September, my visit to Farmington was ending. It was time for me to return to my law practice and
my life in Springfield. My spirits had improved during
the six weeks. I had not resolved the issue of Molly, but
in the loving company of my dear friend and his family,
I was learning to live with uncertainty.

Prior to my arrival, Speed told his mother about my
melancholy. On the evening before I departed, she gave
me a present of an Oxford Bible, which she said was the
best cure for the "blues" if one could take it according
to the truth. I told her I would read it regularly when
I returned home. Parting from my new friends was
difficult. They had received me with open hearts and
cheerful spirits.

My return was brightened because Speed decided
to join me. He planned to close his business interests
in Springfield.

We boarded the steamboat *Lebanon* in Louisville with
the destination of St. Louis. The passage was unevent-
ful, but for a strange experience.

One night, when Speed and I were taking the air on
the top deck, we looked down to see 12 slaves chained
together six and six—like so many fish on a trot line.
Later we learned that a man from Kentucky was trans-
porting them to a farm in the deep South. They were
going to a place where the lash of the master was ruthless and unrelenting.

Yet in their captivity, they were the most cheerful
and apparently happy creatures on board. One played
the fiddle continually, and others danced, sang, cracked
jokes, and played card games.

I could not understand what I was witnessing. How could this be? These slaves were happier in the worst of human conditions than I was as a free man with many blessings in my life.

Chapter Fifteen

If You Make a Bad Bargain

Upon my return to Springfield, my condition was at best tolerable. Though I believed my involvement with Molly was the root of the problem, I continued my resolve not to see her. While I removed myself from social gatherings, she certainly did not. Although she received attention from a number of eligible suitors, she did not appear to favor any of them. It seemed the best course was to immerse myself in my law practice.

Fortunately, a segment from the yearly rhythm of my law practice emerged to take my mind off my personal affairs. For the fall of 1841, no responsibility suited me better than riding my horse from town to town in the 8th Judicial Circuit, arguing cases on debt collection, the destruction of growing crops by unenclosed livestock, or the ownership of a litter of pigs. This was a helpful distraction. I did not have the time or inclination to worry about the central problem in my life.

Because I was on the circuit for the fall, I did not see Speed until I returned to Springfield in November. He had been staying with Hurst who purchased Speed's share of the store. They slept upstairs as Speed and I had for several years.

In early December, I sat with Speed by the fireplace in the store. Hurst was visiting his parents in Alton, and we were alone.

We enjoyed a leisurely morning talking about Speed's family, about the arrangements he made with his financial affairs, the fall social events in Springfield, and the developing attachments among our friends in the Coterie. Rumors were circulating about Conkling and Mercy Levering, and Trumbull and Julia Jayne. Curiously, Speed said nothing of Fanny Henning. Because he did not raise the subject of his engagement, we did not discuss my reticence to see Molly.

Though we were as close as ever, something about Speed was different. He was not his cheerful self. At times, he didn't finish his sentences and glanced off toward the window by the fireplace.

"Something is wrong," I said to him.

"No, it is just that I have not been sleeping well lately."

"And what is causing you to be restless?"

"I don't rightly know."

"No, you do know, and you are choosing not to tell me." He said nothing.

"Have you been feeling melancholy?" I asked him.

He looked down and then replied, "Yes, I have."

"And have you been able to determine a cause?"

"I have."

"Well whatever could it be? You, who have no reason but to feel the greatest joy."

"That is the very cause of it."

"What are you saying? Is it Fanny herself?"

"Yes, it is she."

"No, not you! My despair is as black as night, but you? What cause have you for despair?"

"I don't believe I love her as I should."

"Oh, Speed, how could such doubts assail you? I have good reason for mine, but for you there should be none. Fanny is the sweetest girl alive. She adores you."

He began to explain.

"I wrote my sister that I found more pleasure in the pursuit of something rather than in the attaining of it."

"Why, what is that? It doesn't sound like you at all."

"Matilda rejected me, and I began to think the only pleasure I would ever feel was in the pursuit. I never imagined I would attain someone's love. Now that I have, I am miserable. Perhaps what I wrote my sister is true."

I paused for a moment, looked at his pale and unhappy face, and then continued, "This is utter nonsense. No one is purer than you. You are having the doubts that any man or woman has when marriage nears. There are reasons why it is more pronounced in you."

"What are they?" he asked pointedly.

"I will tell you."

A quizzical look rippled across his face.

"The first cause is that you are naturally of a nervous temperament. I have seen this in you, and it is true of your mother and your brother William."

Speed nodded his assent to this.

"The second cause is bad weather. We have all felt out of sorts this fall. It has been unseasonably hot followed by violent storms and then frigid air."

"Yes, that is possible," he replied.

"The third cause is your intense thought, which twists the sweetest idea into the bitterness of death."

"That is true."

"The fourth cause is the rapid approach of your wedding."

He looked worried and upset by this.

"Lincoln, it may be that I have reasoned myself into a false position."

I stood up, walked toward the window, and looked out it. Then I turned to face him.

"Then let us reason you out of it," I declared.

I walked back and forth as I made my case.

"You say you do not love her as you should. Let us consider the truth or untruth of this statement. Is it not true that you chose to court Fanny rather than 20 others of whom you can think? Is it not true that you did not court her for her wealth? How could you when you knew she had none?

"Is it not true that after you and I had once seen her, you took me all the way to Lexington and back, for no other purpose than to see her again? Is it not true that you chose her for her personal appearance and deportment, and that these impress the heart and not the head? Is it not true that her heavenly black eyes were the basis of your early reasoning on the subject?

"The statement that you do not love her as you should is false, and you must trust your heart over your head."

A wisp of contentment crossed his face, and he said, "I thank you for your kind words."

I replied, "In all likelihood, you will feel those doubts until your marriage in February. It is a tender time for you, and they may grow even stronger, but do not doubt that your Fanny will bring you much happiness."

In January, shortly after our conversation, Speed left for Kentucky. Once again, I buried myself in the law cases represented by Logan and Lincoln.

The tooth, which caused me distress when I visited the Speeds at Farmington, was aching once again. A few days later it was so painful, I couldn't work or sleep. Reluctantly, I decided to go to the dentist. He tore it out with a turnkey, bringing with it a bit of the jaw bone; the consequence of which was that for days my mouth was so sore that I could neither talk nor eat.

The Springfield Washington Temperance Society asked me to give their annual Washington's Birthday address in February. I accepted, and the process of preparing the speech kept me occupied as well.

I did not drink alcohol myself, and I thought carefully about how I wanted to approach the subject. I was interested to learn that many members of the Washington Temperance Society were reformed drunkards. I learned as well that the Washingtonians enjoyed greater success in aiding victims of intemperance than the temperance advocates of the past. Those men, mostly preachers and lawyers, had relied on the harsh tones of denunciation.

The Washingtonians began with sympathy. In winning a man to their cause, they realized they would have to show him they were sincere friends. Abiding by the old maxim that a "drop of honey catches more flies than a gallon of gall," they believed that when human conduct was in need of being influenced, the only approach that would work was persuasion—kind, unassuming persuasion. As this was in line with my own thinking, I decided to make it the heart of my address.

While I was writing the address in late January, I received a letter from Speed. He wrote that, while he was happy to be in the loving company of his family, he was not sharing anything about Fanny with them. Unfortunately this caused his melancholy to deepen, and he even questioned if I was his true friend. Fanny was sick with a fever, and this alarmed him about her health and life. In addition, their wedding would take place on February 15, barely two weeks hence.

I immediately ceased my labors and penned him a response.

First, I forgave him for any doubts he had about our friendship. I reassured him of my feelings for him, and that I felt his sorrows as keenly as I felt my own. I wrote that his concern for Fanny's health and life should banish forever his horrid doubts about the truth of his affection for her. I wondered if the Almighty was testing him for that purpose. He should rejoice at such evidence of his love for her, for if he believed he would meet her death with calm resignation, that would signify he did not love her as he should.

I finished with some addenda about Springfield and posted my response.

On February 9, I received another letter from Speed. He wrote me before receiving my response to his first letter. His concerns were similar to those of his earlier letter, and they had not abated.

Sitting by the fire at Butler's, I responded. I wrote that by the time he received my letter, he would already be married. I was hesitant to advise him, because he would be standing on ground unknown to me.

I hoped he would no longer need comfort from me. But should I be mistaken, and should his joy be blended with occasional distress, I asked him to remember that the unease would pass very shortly. His being happy in Fanny's presence and his intense anxiety about her health convinced me of his deep love for her. If his nerves failed him occasionally, he would soon find balance in his life, and that trouble would be over forever. I hoped that my letter would be a plaster for a place that was no longer sore. With best wishes and respects for both him and Fanny, I ended the letter.

On the night before Speed left for Farmington in January, I had made one request of him. With the wedding on February 15, I asked him to write on the 16th. I would be most anxious to hear from him. He swore that he would honor my wish.

I received the promised one from the 16th. It arrived on the 25th.

I opened it with intense anxiety and trepidation, and read it several times to be sure I understood. It turned out to be better than I expected, so much so that it took me several hours before I became calm. In it, Speed announced that he and Fanny were "no more twain, but one flesh." The wedding had been a blessed and festive occasion—with the support of family and nearby friends. Although Speed wrote he knew his dream of Elysium would never be realized, he had felt no apprehension about any aspect of the day or their future together. He did write that he and Fanny had decided to remain in Kentucky, and they would not be returning to Illinois.

That afternoon, I wrote to Speed once more.

I welcomed his news that meant our forebodings were the worst sort of nonsense. As for never attaining Elysium, it was certainly not the fault of his dear Fanny. I wrote that it was both his and my peculiar misfortune to dream dreams of Elysium far exceeding any earthly possibility. No woman could do more to realize them than Fanny. No one could be unhappy with her. I then told him my old father used to have a saying that, "If you make a bad bargain, hug it the tighter." If by any chance he had made "a bad bargain," it was certainly a more pleasant one than any I could imagine. I was overjoyed for them. I did allow that without them, I should be very lonesome, but I understood that she wished to remain with her family and friends.

A month later, as I was making plans to ride the circuit for the spring session, I received another letter from Speed. This one, above all the others, gave me the greatest joy. For in it, he wrote that his marriage had made him far happier than he ever expected to be. Perhaps Elysium was not a sudden burst of flame, but rather a slow and steady glow.

In my reply, I wrote that his letter gave me more pleasure than I had known in the past year, although I could not be happy until I resolved my dilemma with Molly.

Chapter Sixteen

THE PERSON
I WANTED TO BE

The spring brought another session on the circuit. I found that immersing myself in the affairs of others—and my desire to see them settle their differences if possible—helped me move forward.

I returned to Springfield in June, and in early July, I was greeted with a letter from Speed.

He thanked me for my part in bringing Fanny and him together, and he gently prodded me to reconsider my feelings for Molly. He hoped she might provide me with the happiness that Fanny had brought him.

I wrote him that I was pleased to be thanked, but I wasn't certain I deserved it. I was drawn to it by fate. God made me one of the instruments of bringing Fanny and him together, and He had foreordained their marriage. Whatever God designed for me, He would do it yet. The text by which I decided to live was from Exodus, "Stand still and see the salvation of the Lord."

As for Molly, I wrote that the subject remained painful to me, but before I decided to do one thing or another, I must regain my confidence in my ability to keep my own resolves. I had prided myself in that ability as the chief gem of my character—and I had lost it. Until I regained it, I could not trust myself in any matter of much importance.

August marked the first election day in 10 years that I was not on the ballot. Although I was comfortable with my decision not to run again for the legislature, I felt something was missing from my life. It was also the election in which Douglas won a seat in the US Congress.

An event on August 19 jarred me back into politics.

A letter appeared in the *Sangamo Journal* from Aunt Rebecca of "Lost Townships." Letters from the same person were featured in the *Journal* before, and everyone believed it was the editor, Simeon Francis, writing under the assumed name. In this latest letter, Rebecca, a farmer's wife, discussed the financial crisis in Illinois in a round-about way. The state bank was on the verge of collapse, and the state's currency was almost worthless. The Democrats, who controlled the leadership of the state, were in the unenviable spot of having to inform the people that the state auditor, James Shields, would no longer accept notes from the state bank in payment for state taxes. It fell to Shields to communicate this disastrous news.

Shields was a pleasant, if not cheerful, fellow who was born in Ireland. He was a lawyer and a friend of ours in the Springfield Coterie. His flaws were that he had a fiery temper and a tendency to be vain. He also fancied himself a ladies' man.

While the letter was not unkind to Shields, it did maintain that the governor was going to send instructions to collectors not to take anything but gold and silver for taxes.

When I saw this, I couldn't wait to jump into the fray. This Rebecca letter was insufficient. Here was our chance to vilify the Democrats for their hypocrisy. Here was a state government unwilling to accept the currency from the state's bank for payment of the state's taxes! This called for a humorous, sarcastic invective smuggled into the pages of the *Sangamo Journal* under the name of Aunt Rebecca of the Lost Township. Here was the chance to be the slasher-gaff once more. I was good at it, and I enjoyed doing it. It was time for me to awake from my slumber.

I dashed the letter off in an afternoon.

I had my Aunt Rebecca visiting her neighbor Jeff on his farm. Jeff tells her he can't pay his taxes with the Illinois paper money he's been paid for his crops. The money is worthless.

Rebecca and Jeff track the problem to a proclamation from the state auditor, Jas Shields. Jeff calls Shields "a fool as well as a liar," and that, "with him, truth is out of the question."

Jeff says he saw Shields "among the grandees" and gossiping with all the ladies at a political gathering in Springfield. He describes Shields's affection for all the ladies.

"He was paying his money to this one and that one, and sufferin' great loss because it wasn't silver instead of State paper; and the sweet distress he seemed to be in— his very features, in the ecstatic agony of his soul, spoke audibly and distinctly—'Dear girls, it is distressing, but I cannot marry you all. Too well I know how much you suffer; but do, do remember, it is not my fault that I am so handsome and so interesting.'"

That was the gist of the letter; there were a few more flourishes and window dressings, but I kept it a bit shorter than some of the other anonymous pieces I'd written for the *Journal*.

When I finished, I walked over to Simeon Francis's office and gave him the letter. He published it in the September 2 edition of the *Journal*.

Shields erupted. He was in Quincy on business, but he sent his friend, Gen. Whiteside, to Francis demanding to know the author of the letter. Francis squirmed, tried to deflect the assault, but eventually gave Whiteside my name.

In the September 9 edition of the *Journal*, another Lost Townships letter appeared with a reference to Shields as someone who enjoyed squeezing the hands of the young ladies of Springfield. I didn't write it, and I didn't think Francis wrote it, but I could not think of someone who might have.

On September 15, I rode to Tremont to begin the fall session on the Circuit. The following day, Gen. Whiteside appeared at my inn door to deliver a note from Shields. In Whiteside's presence, I opened the note and read it.

In it, Shields wrote in part:

> Whilst abstaining from giving provocation, I have become the object of slander, vituperation and personal abuse. I take the liberty of requiring a full, positive and absolute retraction of all offensive allusions used by you in these communications, in relation to my private character and standing as a man, as an apology for the insults conveyed in them.
>
> This may prevent consequences which no one will regret more than myself.
> Your ob't servant
> JAS. SHIELDS

I told Whiteside I would have a reply to Shields ready later in the day. In his note, Shields assumed I was the author of all three Lost Townships letters. He believed I was the author of all the insults addressed toward him. For this reason, I wrote that because his note was so full of false assumptions and menace as to consequences, I could not answer it. I gave my note to Whiteside and bade him a safe trip to Springfield.

Two days later, Whiteside returned with a second note from Shields. In this note, Shields clarified his charges, specifying his understanding that I was the author of the Lost Townships letter of September 2. He continued to ask for a complete retraction and wrote that he had no intention of menacing me, but to do himself justice.

While Whiteside waited, I read the note. I returned it to him and said there would be no further negotiation unless Shields withdrew the first note.

When Shields learned this, he sent me a formal challenge.

In 1818, with the adoption of its state constitution, Illinois outlawed dueling, but it was still legal in Missouri. Duels were fought on Bloody Island, a small strip of land in the Mississippi River on the Missouri side, just south of Alton. I was not frightened at the prospect of a duel, but I wanted to avoid it if possible. Once, in the legislature, an opponent almost provoked me into a duel, but we both backed off. If both parties were willing to negotiate, the duel could be averted; however, when one party was unwilling, the other could not retreat without losing honor. I did not wish to fight a duel with Shields, but I could not be degraded in my estimate of myself or my friends.

I chose Dr. Elias Merryman to be my second. General Whiteside served as second for Shields. Their role was to negotiate for Shields and me and to set the terms and conditions of the fight. Shields and I both asked two more friends to be associates for our seconds.

Unfortunately, misunderstandings and missed opportunities occurred as the seconds and associates for both sides tried to lessen the tension. Shields's friends said that if I would explain or apologize, he would withdraw the challenge, but Dr. Merryman insisted that Shields withdraw the challenge first, and then I would explain or apologize. Upon this fine point, the negotiations failed. The date for the duel was set for the afternoon of Thursday, September 22.

I had chosen well when I made my Whig colleague and friend, Albert Bledsoe, one of my associates. On the evening when prospects were bleakest, I visited Bledsoe. Because Shields challenged me, I had the right to choose the weapons for the duel and the manner in which the duel would be fought. Bledsoe counseled me to choose cavalry broadswords. He reasoned that I was eight inches taller than Shields, and my reach exceeded his by three to four inches. Although Shields had served in the military and was probably familiar with the cavalry broadsword, Bledsoe, who attended West Point, offered to train me to use it. My purpose would be to disarm Shields and not to kill him.

Next we designed the space upon which the duel would be fought. We were to stand within the borders of adjacent 6-foot by 10-foot boxes. The boxes would be separated by a 10-foot plank, set into the ground on edge. For crossing the plank, the penalty was death, and for passing beyond the lines of the box, it was surrender.

With these plans and rules in place, Shields and I prepared to fight each other in a duel on Bloody Island. Our seconds would continue discussions until the duel, but no one was optimistic about an agreement. Word of the duel spread through Springfield bringing anticipation and excitement. Caught up in the hubbub, people talked about going to see it. Word came that Shields and I might be arrested, so both camps set out immediately for Alton.

I was accompanied on the way to Alton by Merryman, Bledsoe, Bledsoe's father, and Butler, who was also an associate. Our first assignment was to obtain the broadswords from the cavalry encampment in Jacksonville. When we met the soldiers, and they presented us with a collection of lengthy, lethal weapons, I endeavored to lighten the transaction by telling a story. It reminded me of a soldier who served in the War of 1812. As he left for battle, his darling gave him a bullet pouch with "Victory or Death" sewn into it. He said to her, "Isn't that rather too strong? Suppose you put, 'Victory or Be Crippled.'"

We continued toward Alton when we came upon a diversion. To the side of the trail was a swamp. Further ahead, we came across a horse standing by itself and a farmer trying to pull a large hog out of the mud. He could not do it himself and asked us for help. Merryman insisted we could not spare the time, and he warned me I would be covered with mud. My friends were emphatic we should not stop. I jumped down from my horse and offered to assist. His idea was for me to pull the animal while he pushed it. After several attempts we were successful, and only the bottom quarter of me was mud soaked.

After journeying a little longer, we halted at White Hall. The postmaster, Elliot Lott, was a friend of Merryman's. When he heard of our purpose, he told us he would get word to Hardin to come to Alton as soon as he could. Hardin was someone Shields liked and respected, so Lott believed he might be able to settle the issue.

When we arrived at Alton, the ferry dock was surrounded by a festive crowd of townspeople. Shields and his friends had already arrived and were preparing to board the boat along with the more intrepid citizens.

We would have to wait for the ferry to return for another passage to the island. As we waited, Hardin and Dr. Revel English, a Democrat in the legislature, rode up to the dock with their horses lathering. They were agitated themselves and asked numerous questions about the entire affair.

The ferry returned and we boarded for Bloody Island. Several surgeons accompanied us. The voyage was brief, and we arrived at our destination where Shields's friends had prepared the site for the duel. Merryman dropped the pile of swords by the board that marked the line over which we were not to pass.

As I walked toward the spot where I would soon be fighting Shields, the gravity of the event bore down on me. I really hadn't felt it until that moment. In the company of friends, training with Bledsoe, and getting daily reports from Merryman, it all seemed like a grand adventure. But here I was, perhaps minutes from my death. How had this happened?

From the beginning, it had seemed unreal. Possibly, it was related to my forsaking Molly. If I dishonored myself in abandoning her, perhaps I could regain my honor by fighting for it. The disagreement with Shields now seemed altogether petty. I started it with that fool letter. But that was the way with these things. They started small, one thing led to another, and now I was caught in a web of my own making. Of course, I should apologize to Shields, but it was too late for that.

It was time to practice with the broadsword.

While I slashed away at tree branches and Shields stood quietly watching me, Hardin and English were trying to revive the negotiations. They were in animated discussions with Merryman and Whiteside. What drifted back to me was that Hardin made a proposal that Shields initially rejected. After Dr. Thomas Hope, the editor of the *Democratic Union* in Alton pressured Shields to reconsider, the tide began to turn.

After lengthy discussion with his second and associates, Shields agreed to withdraw his two letters.

I agreed to sign a note to Shields which read, "I did write the 'Lost Township' letter which appeared in the *Journal* of the 2nd, but had no participation, in any form, in any other article alluding to you. I wrote that wholly for political effect. I had no intention of injuring your personal or private character or standing as a man or gentleman. And I will add, that your conduct toward me, so far as I know, has always been gentlemanly; and that I have no personal pique against you, and no cause for any."

With the resolution of the conflict, both sides rejoiced, although some grumbled they would have preferred to see a duel, particularly with broadswords.

A day or two later, I reflected on what had happened.

Two years earlier, after I had "skinned" Thomas, Speed and I had a conversation that I now recalled.

"Lincoln, you must be careful," he'd said.

"Whatever do you mean?" I'd replied

"Do you know Aesop's fables?" he'd asked.

"There isn't one I don't know," I responded.

"The Eagle and the Arrow?"

I'd recited, "A bowman took aim at an eagle and struck him in the heart. As the eagle turned his head in the agony of death, he saw that the arrow was winged with his own feathers. 'How sharper and more painful,' said he, 'are the wounds made by weapons we ourselves have supplied.'"

"Lincoln, you must be careful," he'd repeated.

The contretemps with Shields started with my rash behavior. I rushed with deep delight to be the slasher-gaff once more. It was not the only example, just the latest one. Speed may have been right that the appearance had become the reality. I had enjoyed the power to hurt my political opponents.

It was time to ask if this was the person I wanted to be.

Chapter Seventeen

A Matter
of Profound Wonder

"Molly," I said, "I did not know you wrote poetry."

"Oh, Mr. Lincoln," she replied, "Do not flatter me."

"No, no," I said, looking at her intently, "Do not devalue yourself. Your verses have merit."

I quoted, "Ye jews-harps awake, the Auditor's won— Rebecca, the widow, has gained Erin's son."

She followed, "The pride of the north from the emerald Isle.

Has been woo'd and won by a woman's sweet smile:

    The combat's relinquished, old love's all forgot,

    To the widow he's bound, oh! bright be his lot;"

We were sitting across from each other at a table on the evening of Nettie Hardin's wedding in Jacksonville. It was September 27, five days after my confrontation with Shields. I was seated between Sarah Rickard and Molly, both of whom were unescorted.

Hardin, who had intervened successfully at the duel, brought us together on the occasion of his sister's marriage. He was a cousin of Molly's and was trying to further her interest as well as mine.

I turned toward Molly and asked, "Did I hear that you wrote the third Lost Township letter?"

"Yes, Julia and I both had a hand in it. The poem that came the next week was mine."

"I have heard that as well."

"We had no idea it would lead to your encounter with Mr. Shields. You defended yourself ably."

"Perhaps, but I have relied on your cousins in my brief time in Springfield. First Stuart, then Logan, and now Hardin."

"But you were willing to risk your life for your honor—and to defend mine for what I wrote."

"I wish I could lay claim to that, but the truth is Shields was most vexed with the foolishness of my letter."

"Now it is you who lessen yourself unfairly. We all wrote foolish prattle."

"Shields was irate because he cannot keep his temper, and he does fancy himself a favorite among the ladies, but my attack on him was unprovoked. I could hardly hide behind my letter as a political 'set-off' when Shields had not attacked me. I was fortunate Hardin and the others could prevail upon him to accept the terms of my apology."

"Well, our admiration for you is not diminished in the slightest because you are forthright and honorable."

That night many of us stayed overnight in the spacious quarters of Hardin's farmhouse. The following morning I came out to find the others had started on a ride—some in carriages and the others on horseback. Molly was sitting on the porch, downcast, because as an unaccompanied young woman, she was not welcomed by the others.

"Come, Molly," I exclaimed to her. "We shall find them and join their adventure!"

That was the beginning of our reacquaintance.

It continued for several weeks. Eliza and Simeon Francis, who still believed Molly and I would make a happy couple despite our earlier missteps, opened the parlor of their house for us to meet. We kept our meetings secret from everyone else in Springfield. We were direct and honest with each other. She asked me if Matilda had rejected me, and I told her I could not bring myself to propose to her. She asked why not, and I told her I wasn't sure.

The letters which Speed and I exchanged, and the feelings they unearthed, caused me to reflect on my courtship of Molly. Oddly, Speed's reticence to marry Fanny and his doubts about whether he loved her deeply enough paralleled my own doubts and fears about Molly. Now, as I began to feel more fondly toward her, they rose again to plague me.

I told her once more that I could not buy even a modest house for us, and that we would begin our married life in a single room at the Globe Tavern. She said she could be happy there, but I did not believe it. I asked her to imagine the space if two became three, and she just smiled.

We were very different. Because she was so attentive and engaging when we were courting, I did not focus on our particularities. Would our temperaments be compatible? Her anger ran deeper than mine. I had only seen flashes of her temper, but there were stories of it. She was reputed to be irritable and willful, but I had not seen that side of her. If it were true, surely it could be no worse than my melancholy. I lived with it by simply withdrawing. Would we understand each other when we were troubled? Her sister Elizabeth now opposed our marriage because we were such different people, and Ninian never favored it because he believed Mary would be marrying beneath herself.

I kept coming back to the simple question of whether I loved her sufficiently to become her husband. She loved me sufficiently to become my wife. She had proven that. For a year and a half, she had lived with the hope that we would reconcile. She had not seen anyone else regularly during that time. I could not doubt her love.

If I could not answer the question of my feelings for her, there was another aspect of the choice. For eighteen months I had suffered from my inability to keep my pledge to Molly. It brought constant and, sometimes deep, melancholy. The gem of my character was tarnished. My word was no longer good. It killed my soul. If I were to marry Molly, I could live with myself again. Perhaps it was time for me to listen to my father. If I were making a bad bargain, it was up to me to hug it all the more.

Caught in this dilemma, I decided to resolve it as I had the others. I would consult with Speed by letter.

On October 5, I wrote him about the duel with Shields, but then I turned to what was deeply troubling me.

"The immense suffering you endured from the first days of September till the middle of February you never tried to conceal from me, and I well understood. You have now been the husband of a lovely woman nearly eight months. That you are happier now than the day you married her I well know; for without, you would not be living. But I want to ask a closer question—Are you now in feeling as well as judgment, glad you are married as you are? Please answer it quickly as I feel impatient to know."

Three weeks later, Speed wrote, "Do not hesitate or longer doubt that happiness will be the result of your marriage. I found contentment once Miss Henning and

I had finally made up and determined to risk our happiness in each other's keeping."

A few days later, in the parlor at the Francis' house, I told Molly that I could marry her.

She was overjoyed, and we spent the afternoon planning our wedding. We both decided that we would not tell a soul. No one would be given the chance to dissuade us. I would ask Charles Dresser, an Episcopal priest, to marry us at his house on November 4. If he agreed, Molly would inform Elizabeth and Ninian on the day of our wedding. She chose Julia Jayne and Anna Rodney for bridesmaids, and my choice for groomsmen was Jim Matheny and Beverly Powell. We would let them know at noon on our wedding day.

On the morning of November 4, Mary told Elizabeth of our plans. Elizabeth was stunned, and when Ninian declared that no Todd would be married anywhere but in his house, Elizabeth complained there was no time to prepare. She said she could offer nothing but gingerbread and beer. Molly replied that would be fine.

At Butler's house that morning, I was dressed in my finest clothes and blacking my boots. All the preparations caused me to feel a bit out of sorts. When Butler's young son pestered me by asking where I was going, I replied, "To hell, I reckon."

As the day progressed, I mellowed a bit, but on our walk from Butler's to the Edwards' house, Jim Matheny said I looked like I was going to the slaughter, and I better cheer up before we reached our destination.

When we arrived, we learned the ceremony would be in the parlor where Molly and I had courted two years before. Molly wanted this to be a surprise for me. Reverend Dresser, wearing his clerical vestments, was joined by State Supreme Court Justice Thomas Browne, a man noted for speaking his mind. Friends and family were already standing in the parlor, waiting for Molly and me. At first, people seemed a little stiff, but this was no doubt due to the suddenness of the event. I heard whispers of what I supposed was polite gossip and saw an occasional raised eyebrow.

When Julia and Anna, wearing festive dresses, prepared to enter the parlor, the crowd rose to attention. A violin soloist played a lovely piece by Vivaldi, and Molly entered the room in a white satin wedding dress on the arm of her brother-in-law Ninian.

After the Bible readings, we gave our vows to each other, and Rev. Dresser asked me to place the ring on Molly's finger. Choosing the ring was one thing I had done in advance. On the inside of it, I asked the jeweler to engrave, "A.L. to Mary, Nov. 4, 1842. Love is Eternal."

As I placed it on Molly's finger, I said, "With this ring I thee endow with all my goods and chattels, lands and tenements."

At this, Judge Browne blurted, "Lord Jesus Christ, God Almighty, Lincoln, the Statute fixes all that."

Reverend Dresser recovered, smiled, and pronounced us man and wife.

Speed was right. The first days of our marriage were filled with happiness. Our room in the Globe Tavern was cheerful and cozy. In that simple setting, we relaxed and let time stop for the moment. A week later, finishing a letter to my friend, Samuel Marshall, I wrote, "Nothing

new here, except my marrying, which to me, is a matter
of profound wonder."

My marriage marked a transition in my life. It was
the end of one stage and the beginning of another. I
came to Springfield unfamiliar with the customs of
a large town which was on the verge of becoming a
small city. I was a novice lawyer and apprenticing as
a politician. My mentors, Stuart and Logan, and my
new friends Speed, Baker, Hardin, and Douglas were
educated and cultured. While I had progressed in my
self-education, I would never be their equal. I was not
at ease with women. Courtship was a mystery. There
was so much I didn't know or understand that brought
doubt and uncertainty.

Five years after I arrived in 1837, I had established
myself in Springfield. Under the tutelage of Stuart and
Logan, I had become a successful lawyer. After four
terms in the legislature, I was a leader in the Whig Party.
Through my friendship with Speed and the others, I was
accepted into the Springfield Coterie. One of its members was now my wife.

I owed this to my driving ambition to better myself
and to be worthy of a strange presentiment I had of
purpose in my life. At times, I feared my ambition, like
Macbeth's, could consume me. On the surface, it did
not appear so, particularly compared to Douglas's, but
underneath, it was fierce and unrelenting. The problem
was to keep it from tainting me. Molly was as ambitious
as I, perhaps more so. If I wished for more outward success, and surely I did, Molly was the partner I needed.

In my five years in Springfield, I learned that while

I enjoyed aspects of the law, politics was more fulfilling. But there, as well, lurked danger. To succeed in politics, I had to use guile. I had to delay and compromise. I had to trim and obfuscate. Could I do this and remain true to myself? All this brought me back to the discussion Speed and I had after seeing the performance of Macbeth. In politics, one had to maneuver between appearance and reality. Could I alter the appearance and be true to the reality? That was the dilemma I faced.

From the day I asked Molly to release me from my promise until the day we were married, for those eighteen months, my life was a living hell. Melancholy was my steady and unyielding companion. I could not free myself from its hold. With my marriage, it eased away. My resolve was re-established. My word was good. I held true to the pledge I had given Molly two years earlier. In Speed's words, I was willing to risk my happiness in the care of another. I was once again comfortable with myself.

Part Four

Chapter Eighteen

Turnabout is Fair Play

Molly and I adapted to our life in the Globe Tavern. Although the room was small, it was cozy. The furnishings were simple: a bed, bureaus for each of us, two small tables, and accompanying armchairs. Sarah Beck, the manager of the Tavern, kindly offered us the same room where Molly's sister Frances and her husband Dr. William Wallace lived for three years after their marriage. They had just moved out.

It cost four dollars a week to stay at the Tavern. As a new bride, Mary was spared cooking, cleaning, and laundry. It was all included in our fee. A pleasant dining area meant that boarders lingered after meals and became quite familiar with each other. Albert Bledsoe, to whom I owed the advice of challenging Shields with the cavalry broadsword, was also a boarder at the Globe Tavern.

We were located on Adams Street, just two blocks from the town square and the capitol. It was a short walk to the office of Lincoln & Logan on Hoffman Row. Molly and I enjoyed taking leisurely walks through the streets of Springfield. I had a new companion for what had previously been a solitary pleasure.

One afternoon, we were walking arm in arm around the town square. Molly slowed, glanced at the capitol, and then turned to look up at me.

"Husband," she said proudly, "Stuart is giving up his seat in Congress. Will you run for it?"

"I will."

"You will have opposition?"

"Yes, Hardin and Baker."

"They are our good friends. Will that make it more difficult?"

I didn't reply and then asked, "What do you think?"

"Baker is more outgoing and energetic. He is very ambitious, second only to Douglas. He will throw himself into the race."

"He has been my close friend ever since I descended from our office to rescue him in the court chamber."

Molly added, "Cousin John is more distant and less demonstrative, but he will organize effectively."

"He rescued me from harm at the hand of Shields, and he was the one who reunited us."

"You may hold back and make the mistake of believing your contributions in the legislature entitle you to the nomination."

I countered, "I have strong support in the party."

"Yes, but you must pursue the office vigorously."

"I wish to go to Washington as much as you."

"When will it be decided?" she asked.

"Baker and I will contest for the votes of the Sangamon County Whigs in March. Whoever wins their endorsement will go up against Hardin at the District Convention in May."

"Then you must defeat Baker in March."

Just before Christmas, we returned to the warmth of our room after a bracing afternoon walk. Draping my legs over the comforter, I sat down on the bed, while Molly settled into one of the armchairs. Perhaps it was the approaching holidays and the family gatherings they would bring or the effect of an hour of vigorous exercise, but her face radiated a distinct glow.

She asked, "Did you notice the nativity scene in the window of Irwin's Dry Goods?"

I had not paid particular attention to it.

"No, I did not."

"Oh, husband, you are always wrapped up in your own thoughts. You didn't notice that I stopped and looked at it for a while."

"I did notice, but I thought you were looking at the lovely red gown next to it."

"Oh, heavens no, although I did notice it. How can you be so dull-witted."

I was completely confused.

"Mr. Lincoln, we will soon be three."

I was momentarily stunned, but rose immediately to greet her with a kiss as she stood by the chair like a blooming rose. I hugged her closely, and all I could say was, "Oh Molly, how blessed we are."

We were to become a family, and I would be a father. For someone who was so hesitant to marry, I was awestruck by the changes in my life. I had given myself up to the current of a river and accepted the flow that was taking me further downstream. I had been the child of a father who did not understand me. Now it would be my turn to be a father. I resolved to build the tie of love with our children. I looked forward to playing with them.

The campaign for Stuart's congressional seat heated up in March. Baker and I were competing arduously for the support of the Sangamon County Whigs. As there were few policy differences between us, the choice turned to personal preference. I was quite certain my devotion to the Whig Party would be the deciding factor.

Baker's supporters launched an unusual attack on me. Given my connection with the Todd family, they portrayed me as a Springfield aristocrat who was out of touch with the people. When I first learned of this, I thought it so ludicrous, it was not worthy of reply. When it caught on, I was surprised and angry. I took Jim Matheny aside and told him, "Jim, I am now and always shall be the same Abe Lincoln that I always was."

On March 20, in polling that lasted most of the day, the Sangamon Whigs chose to endorse Baker or me to run for the congressional seat. In the morning, support for Baker was strong. His forceful campaign brought him what appeared to be a decisive lead. After a surge of Baker votes just before noon, his lieutenants urged me to withdraw.

I declined and decided to discuss it with my key backers. After debating it thoroughly, we concluded that I would not have enough support to overcome Baker's lead. I congratulated him and withdrew from the contest. Unfortunately, we could not have foreseen that most of my voters would appear in the late afternoon. By the end of the day, the vote was close, but I had already conceded earlier in the day.

When I returned to the Globe Tavern late that afternoon, Molly was eager to hear the outcome.

"What?" she cried, "You withdrew?"

"Yes, it seemed clear he would win easily."

"But wasn't it supposed to be close?" she asked angrily.

"I was disappointed, and it didn't occur to me that Baker's people would vote early and mine would come later."

"The farmers and laborers support you. Of course they'd come later."

"I should have known."

"They support you despite that foolishness of being connected to my family. They distrust Baker because they know his wife is a very rich woman."

"No, Molly, I didn't think of any of that."

"And then they preyed on your sense of honor," she said harshly.

"I suppose so," I mumbled.

"You must be more distrustful."

"I suppose so."

"It's not in your nature, which is too full of kindness. They may seem like honorable men, but underneath they are snakes. They took advantage of you."

I said nothing.

Rising from the armchair and gripping the back of it tightly, she glared fiercely at me. She was merciless and agitated.

"You cannot let this happen again," she cried. "You must let your ambition drive you harder. Baker has energy and determination. He campaigned every day. You did not. You were too sure you would win. I know your passion runs deeper, but you must pursue it with more feverish purpose."

I had never seen her like this. Was it the force of new life within her or a side of her she had held back?

Though I was startled and unsettled, I composed myself and said, "You are right."

This calmed her, and then she asked "What comes next?"

"On May 1st, the district convention will choose the Whig candidate. The contest will be close, but I believe Hardin will win."

"And he will win the election?'"

"I believe he will."

"And then your political ambitions will be finished?"

I looked down and said nothing.

"Are they?" she demanded with rising intensity.

"Perhaps not. I have an idea that I will put before the convention."

"What is it?"

"Since there is limited opportunity for rising leaders in the Whig Party to serve in Congress, I will propose that the seat in the Whig district be rotated among us. In 1844, Hardin will be succeeded by Baker. After Hardin and Baker, it will be my turn. Turnabout will be fair play."

"And you do not anticipate foul play?"

"If the convention adopts the proposal, I think that would be difficult."

"Let us hope, Mr. Lincoln," she said with determination, "that you are successful."

The delegates at the Pekin convention chose Hardin to run as the Whig nominee for congress. Before his nomination was formally approved, I offered my proviso to the convention. Although the Hardin supporters were not enthusiastic, the Baker delegates joined my friends in voting for it. It was adopted and became known as the Pekin accord.

Molly was pleased with the result, although she pointed out that Baker was named in the proposal adopted by the convention, and I was not. I told her what was important was that the principle had been established. In the August 1843 election, Hardin won the congressional seat.

On August 1, 1843, in our room in the Globe Tavern, attended by her uncle John Todd and my friend Dr. Anson Henry, Molly gave birth to a baby boy. I had deferred to her on naming our child, and her choice was Robert Todd Lincoln after her father. We would come to know him as Bobby. It was hard to believe that Molly and I could love each other any more than we did at that moment. To see our little one, the union of our flesh and spirit, was to believe in God's blessings in this life.

Chapter Nineteen

I Conducted Myself with Equanimity

While Hardin served in Congress, my life in Springfield settled into a comfortable rhythm. Although the caseload at Logan and Lincoln was always full, I continued to practice on the circuit in the spring and the fall. My income was increasing, but I began to chafe at dividing our earnings by two-thirds for Logan and one-third for me.

Molly was a doting mother for our baby boy, and I enjoyed being a father. When Bobby cried from colic, I would carry him in a towel on my shoulder throughout the Globe Tavern, trying my best to soothe him. If I swayed gently, talked softly, or hummed a tune, he calmed down.

In the fall of 1843, we moved to a small rental cottage at 214 South Fourth Street. We hoped our stay there would be temporary as we were beginning to search for a house in which to settle permanently.

On January 16, 1844, we purchased a one-and-a-half story house at Eighth and Jackson from the Reverend Charles Dresser for $1,500. The house was special to us, for two years earlier, I had visited it when I asked Rev. Dresser to marry us. We moved into our new house in May.

The house at Eighth and Jackson was a warm and welcoming home for Molly and me. In her youth, because of her father's hasty remarriage and in a house with 13 siblings, Molly had known uncertainty and doubt. For this reason, she wanted to create a loving home for her husband and her children. She welcomed the roles of cooking, cleaning, and washing our clothes.

There were, however, times when Molly's temper flared. She hired local young women to help with the cooking and sewing. If the meat was tough because it had been boiled too long or if a repaired seam came unstitched, she railed at the girl and threatened to beat her. My cousin Harriet Hanks stayed with us to attend Springfield Female Seminary, and in return she helped with the chores. Molly thought Harriet was lazy and scolded her frequently. The disputes between them worsened during Harriet's short stay. Sometimes Molly's anger was directed at me. When she screamed, "Mr. Lincoln, do not wrestle with your son on our parlor floor," and armed herself with the coffee pot, I simply left the house and spent a peaceful hour or two in the library at the capitol.

In 1844, another significant change was brought to my life. In November, Logan told me he would like to form a partnership with his son David. We agreed to a pleasant parting, and I decided to establish my own firm. For my partner, I chose William H. Herndon. Billy, as I had always called him, was 10 years younger than I. I'd known him from my early days in Springfield, and we had grown fond of each other. I had valued so many mentors in my life that I looked forward to being a mentor for Billy.

Logan and I had moved our office from Hoffman Row to the second floor of the Tinsley building, a new structure Seth Tinsley built on the southwest corner of Adams and Sixth Streets. It was across the street from the capitol. When Billy and I began our practice, we chose the third floor of the Tinsley building.

Closing down the records at Logan and Lincoln, I came across a thin file marked "Stuart and Lincoln: unresolved." The only case left was the suit the Andersons

brought against General Adams for what they alleged
was the theft of their land. The previous summer,
I wrote and dated a note that General Adams recently
died, and three months later the court abated the lawsuit. At the time, I did not know if the Andersons were
still living, but I wrote them a letter apprising them that
their lawsuit had come to naught. It was my sad duty to
write a note to file that I never heard back from them.

Although reluctant to give up his seat in Congress,
Hardin observed the terms of the Pekin accord and
informed the newspapers he would not run for re-elec-
tion. At the Whig convention in the late spring of 1844,
Baker was nominated to run for congress. The following
August, he won the general election and left for Washington to serve in the 29th Congress.

During Baker's term, war began with Mexico. It
started with the annexation of Texas in March, 1845,
and its admission as a state the following December.
Mexico had never recognized Texas as an independent
territory. When tensions rose over a border dispute,
President Polk ordered soldiers led by Zachary Taylor
to protect American interests in southern Texas. Many
of us Whigs thought Polk, a Democrat, was trying to
provoke a war with Mexico to take territory it was unwilling to sell.

In the fall of 1845, I took the first steps in my campaign for the Whig congressional nomination in the
next election. I began with a visit to Baker at his office
in Springfield. We greeted each other cheerfully. We had
never allowed political differences or ambition to inter-
fere with our deep friendship. The afternoon sunshine

flowed through the windows into elongated patches on the wood floor. We had chosen the late afternoon hour so we could be alone. Baker invited me to sit with him at a green-covered table. The chairs were comfortable.

"You have come to learn my plans," he said with a light smile and the hint of a chuckle.

"Although the election is nearly a year away, I need to start organizing," I replied.

"Yes, all those details I've never been any good at. Give me the stump, and I'll speak all day, but spare me the rest of it."

"Hardin is better at it than either of us."

"I hear he might like to run again."

"What are your plans?"

"More direct than usual, my old friend," he laughed.

"It would be helpful if I knew."

"It would also be helpful if I knew," he laughed again, and then he added, "but here's what I think. You deserve the chance. It's what we agreed to in Pekin."

I'm sure my face showed the relief I felt. I knew it would be difficult for him to yield the seat. I did hope that he would abide by the principle of the Pekin accord, and I was grateful for his decision.

"But there's one thing," he continued. "If Hardin gets back in, all bets are off. I'd probably get back in just to spite him."

"Well, I hope that won't happen."

"And there's something else. If this thing with Mexico gets worse, there will be war. In which case, I'll round up a regiment and head south. Someone else can serve out the rest of this term."

On March 10, 1846, we had another joyous event in our lives—the birth of our second son, Edward Baker Lincoln. We named him after Baker, of whom Mary was also very fond. We decided to call him Eddie. Eddie looked like he would be long and tall like me, whereas Bobby was short and low like a Todd.

Bobby was delighted to have a little brother. He couldn't wait for him to be big enough to play with us. When he was, Bobby and I would have a new companion as we took walks around the neighborhood and had adventures pretending to be pirates.

Shortly after Eddie's birth, Hardin asked me to visit him at his farm in Jacksonville. It was a warm, early spring day, and we were able to sit outside on the porch where I had encountered Molly the morning she had been left behind by her friends in the Springfield Coterie. I had fond memories of many of the parties at Hardin's farm.

A cool breeze swept over us, and the birds flew by looking for debris with which to build their nests.

"The blue jays choose the same spot every year," Hardin observed "It's over there underneath that rafter. They are raucous, but we put up with them."

"Not unlike the Democrats," I replied

"Yes, that's good, Lincoln. I gather they will put up the Reverend Peter Cartwright for the congressional seat. What kind of bird is he like?"

"If I had to say, I think a blue jay is a good fit, but maybe a great horned owl is better. He has a rather severe look to him."

"And whom do you think is best suited to trim his tufts?"

Looking him directly in the eye, I said, "I would like the chance to do that."

"I have given it considerable thought, and I have invited you here to tell you that I will run for the seat. I am the best person to oppose him. I have the experience, and I won't let him goad me in debate. Since you are a scoffer and I am a member of a church, he will not be able to claim you are unfit for office."

I had expected this so I asked him calmly, "What about the Pekin accord?"

"I am not legally or morally bound by it. Baker was named in the resolution, but not you. Since Baker's election, the field is open again."

"You don't acknowledge that 'turnabout is fair play?'"

"Not when nominating an infidel who will lose the election. You must think of the Whig Party. Cartwright will shred you for your heretical views. Unfortunately too many people know about them."

"It will not be an issue, and if it were, I would answer honestly."

"Then you would most certainly lose."

This angered me, and it cut deeper because it came from my friend.

I rose from my chair and walked across the porch to steady myself. Turning to confront him, I raised my voice.

"I am dismayed that you are telling me this. You were one of my first friends in Springfield. You rushed to Alton to save me from my foolishness with Shields. You encouraged Molly and me to marry."

I had to be careful not to let my rage boil, but I glowered at him.

"It was Molly who warned me of this. It was she who said, 'They are snakes.' I have always trusted you. And now you are stabbing me in the back. How can you betray me?"

"I am only doing what is best for the Party."

"This is not true. You are sacrificing our friendship to do what is best for you. You are putting your ambition ahead of your honor. You have become Macbeth."

I finished by saying, "I will run against you and do all I can to defeat you."

This time I would not lose to Hardin for lack of effort.

His first feint was to propose that I run for governor, a thankless task in a Democratic state, and we returned the favor by proposing that he run for governor himself.

The foundation of my campaign was the Pekin accord. Hardin had stepped aside for Baker, and Baker for me because he said it was my turn. This was the way to give ambitious young Whigs the chance to serve in congress. We three had agreed to it.

I had six months to gain as much support as I could in the district, and I used every opportunity. When I practiced on the circuit, I buttonholed all the Whigs in town. I met with newspaper editors to ask for their endorsements. I twisted the arms of state senators and representatives. Molly, who was aghast at the treachery of her cousin, joined me at campaign events and charmed reluctant Whigs.

It became a question of who could line up more support. Gradually, my strategy began to work. More and more Whig leaders, though partial to Hardin, turned toward me because of our agreement to rotate congressional terms. They also recognized all the work I had done for the Whig Party over the years.

I made it clear to my supporters that they were to say nothing negative about Hardin. If we were to win the nomination, we would need his backers to win the general election.

Ever so gradually I began to gain the advantage, and at the district convention in Petersburg on May 1, 1846, I was nominated as the Whig candidate for US Congress.

My Democratic opponent in the general election was the Rev. Peter Cartwright, a renowned Methodist preacher and circuit rider. He was 24 years older than I.

Cartwright was both a religious leader and a politician. He had served two terms in the legislature; in his victory in 1832 for his second term, he defeated me. Large and imposing, with a fervent belief in God's will and Andrew Jackson's politics, Cartwright was a forceful, and sometimes divisive, figure in central and southern Illinois. Ironically, Cartwright, who was a gifted orator, had the reputation for being an ineffective campaigner.

I spoke in almost every town and village in the district. I left Billy in charge of our law firm, and I did not take a case for the duration of the campaign.

Because war with Mexico was declared on May 13, 1846, the newspapers were filled with dispatches and articles about the war. Hardin volunteered, and, having served as a leader in the state militia, he became colonel of the First Illinois Volunteers. Baker resigned from Congress and took charge of the Fourth Illinois

Regiment. My race with Cartwright for Baker's seat in Congress was not regarded as newsworthy.

The campaign drifted along listlessly through the heat of June and July.

I happened to be in the office on an afternoon in mid-July. Billy had stepped out for lunch.

When he returned, he was in a frenzy.

"What has happened now?" I asked.

"Mr. Lincoln, we've learned that Cartwright is spreading innuendo and rumors about you in the northern counties."

"What are the charges this time?"

"That you are an infidel and an open scoffer of Christianity. He is trying to turn the Christian Whigs against you."

"What do our colleagues think we should do about it?"

"They think it is best to ignore it."

"Well, they may be right, and then again, they may not. Let's give it a day or two and see what we think."

The problem with Cartwright's whispering campaign was that Whigs in the southern counties might begin to believe it. If they did, we could be in trouble.

I told Billy I would prepare the text of a handbill and read it to him the following morning. The next day found him bright and eager to hear what I had written. I read parts of it to him:

> A charge having got into circulation in some of the neighborhoods of this district, in substance that I am an open scoffer at Christianity, I have by the advice of some friends concluded to notice the subject in this form. That I am not a mem-

ber of any Christian Church, is true; but I have
never denied the truth of the Scriptures; and I
have never spoken with intentional disrespect of
religion in general, or of any denomination of
Christians in particular.

I concluded by saying, "I do not think I could myself,
be brought to support a man for office, whom I knew to
be an open enemy of, and scoffer at, religion."

When I finished, Billy seemed perplexed and asked,
"Mr. Lincoln, is it true?"

"Well, Billy, we may have argued over a passage or
two from the Scriptures, but ninety percent of it is true,
and that's good enough."

We published the handbill on July 31, just three days
before the election.

It turned out that Cartwright had made a mistake
that backfired on him. His jab at me about religion
caused many voters to reaffirm their commitment to the
separation of church and state, and for some to come to
the conclusion that they did not want to be represented
in Congress by a firebrand Methodist preacher.

On election day, I received 6,340 votes; 4,829
votes were cast for Cartwright. It was the most sub-
stantial victory for a Whig congressional candidate
in the district. Though I would not take my seat until
December of 1847, I was elected to the Congress of
the United States.

Three months after the election, I wrote Speed,
"Being elected to Congress, though I am very grateful
to our friends for having done it, has not pleased me as
much as I expected."

Perhaps it was depleted energy from the rigorous campaign, or because it would be almost a year and a half before I left for Washington, or achieving a goal and being ambitious for a higher one. Because the election gave the Democrats a majority in the state legislature, Douglas would become a US Senator; whatever I achieved, Douglas was always a step ahead of me.

Looking back on the nominating process and the campaign for the House seat, I could say that I conducted myself with equanimity. This was new for me. Under the pressure of attacks in the past, I responded with equal or greater parts of vengeance. In this campaign, when Hardin betrayed me and Cartwright accused me of being an infidel, where I would have skinned them or resorted to the slasher-gaff, I forbore. It was a political presence with which I was growing more comfortable.

Late one night, several months after my election, I was at the capitol library. I'd walked there after dinner to research a case but stayed on to read the newspapers. At midnight, it was time to return home.

As I opened the huge front door, I could barely see ahead of me. While I was reading, a heavy, thick fog had descended on Springfield. It was as if a dark thundercloud covered the streets around the capitol. As our house on Eighth and Jackson was only four blocks away, I set out into the dense, swirling vapor.

The front steps were hardly recognizable. I almost stumbled. After a few strides, I looked up and could not see the capitol. I began to wonder if I was walking in the right direction. I couldn't recognize the shapes and distinguishing features of the nearby buildings. How foolish I'd been to stay so late. I did not know if I was walking toward my home or away from it.

As I struggled with my fright, a few feet ahead, I saw what might be the entrance to one of Springfield's many alleys. In the murk and gloom before me, I thought I saw the form of another person ever so gradually taking shape. I could not tell if it was real or not. Was it a white-haired hag dressed in black? I could not tell. And then, from a thin, watery voice, diffused through the swirling mist, came what I could clearly recognize as words, words spoken to me....

> Tall thin man,
> Why dress in black?
> Do you mourn
> For what you lack?
>
> Do not seek
> The lesser crown
> Office great
> Will bring renown
>
> Fortune's price
> The land aflame
> Blood and death
> Upon your name

"Who are you?" I cried, but the phantom figure dissolved into the night. The fog was too thick for me to pursue it. Though the words made no immediate sense, I tried to remember them.

I was able to find my way home. Molly and the boys were asleep. I sat down in my favorite chair in the living room and stirred the fire to life. The verses repeated themselves to me. What could they mean? I had no idea. Perhaps Molly could help me make some sense of them. I leaned back and fell into a deep and fitful sleep.

Chapter Twenty

DAZZLING BY ITS GLITTER, POMP, AND PAGEANTRY

I awoke to the strong smell of coffee. Molly was standing next to me with a cup and saucer. She had built and started the fire, warmed the pot, and begun the morning chores.

"For you, husband," she said.

Her face slipped into an expression of deep concern.

"Why have you slept in that chair?" she asked. "You look frightful."

I told her of my unsettling walk home, the weird apparition, and the mysterious prophecy.

Molly was just as incredulous as I. She sat down in the adjacent chair. We were silent for awhile. Finally I spoke.

"If I saw anyone at all, it must have been one of those madwomen who roam our streets at night."

"Was it the same one you've seen before?"

"It may have been, but the fog was so thick I couldn't tell if it was a person."

"But who spoke the words?"

"She must have, but the words are meaningless."

Molly didn't reply, but I could tell from her face that she didn't agree.

She then asked, "Do you think anyone can tell the future?"

"I don't think so, but there are seers who say they can."

"Could this woman be one of them?"

"Why would you think that?"

"'Tall thin man,'—that could be you."

"Or one hundred other men in Springfield."

"Dressed in black?"

"So are they," I added, "and what is it I lack? I've just been elected to Congress."

"But why have you felt so dissatisfied since the election?"

"Perhaps it's because I am always thinking of Douglas. He is ahead of me in the race of ambition."

"Do not doubt yourself, Mr. Lincoln. The verses from this madwoman may be telling us that you and Douglas are connected. The 'lesser crown' may be a seat in Congress. 'Office great' must be the Senate. It means you will challenge Douglas for his senate seat."

"Douglas will become powerful in the senate," I said. "I do not believe I will ever be able to defeat him, but even if I could, what do those last words mean? Whichever of us prevailed would be ill-fated. We would be part of some great tragedy."

Molly thought carefully about this. Then she said, "We cannot tell the future. We can only see that you and Douglas have parts to play. We can see that you and he will clash for an 'office great,' but that is as much as we can know."

"Unless it is meaningless and has nothing to do with either of us."

The prolonged wait before traveling to Washington was hard on all of us. I could immerse in my law cases and travel the circuit, but Molly was anxious to begin her new life. Unlike most congressional wives, she and the children would be traveling with me to Washington. She envisioned a life of balls and elaborate parties. As she had been in Springfield, she imagined herself at the center of the social world of Washington.

On March 25, 1847, the headline "Dreadful Battle" appeared in the *Sangamo Journal*. The article was a report on the Battle of Buena Vista, which was fought in Mexico on February 22–23. Shortly after war was declared, General Zachary Taylor led a brilliant campaign, fighting battle after battle where he was outnumbered by the Mexican Army. At Buena Vista, Taylor's army of 4,600 defended a mountain pass against Santa Anna's 15,000 men. They were almost overrun, but held on for a stirring victory that was celebrated across the country.

A week later, I returned home from the office where Billy and I worked all day long preparing declarations for our cases. When I entered through the front door, I saw Bobby sitting on our parlor sofa next to his mother trying to comfort her. She was weeping and appeared to have dropped a letter, the pages of which lay scattered on the floor.

I kneeled down beside her and stretched my arm around Bobby.

"Molly, what is it?"

Her weeping did not abate.

"Molly, what can we do for you?"

Bobby and I could do nothing to ease her distress.

My eye was drawn to the letter. I could keep my arm around Bobby, who had nestled close to me, and reach for it. I saw by the signature that it was from Martinette Hardin, my friend Hardin's sister.

I located the first page and began to read.

> My dearest Molly,
>
> I can hardly bring myself to write you such sad tidings.
>
> My dear brother John, whom we all adored, was killed in the Battle of Buena Vista on February

23. May he rest with the angels.

We have learned that he died bravely.

He and his men were in the center of the battle.

One of them wrote that before the fighting he told them, "Soldiers! You have never met an enemy, but you are now in front. I know the 1st Illinois will never fail. I will ask no man to go where I will not lead."

They held their position under a fierce artillery attack. Santa Anna himself led his men forward—on foot, after his horse was shot from under him.

After nine hours, Santa Anna raised a black flag. There would be no surrender.

John yelled to his men, "Remember Illinois— give them the blizzard, boys! It comes to victory or death."

He was surrounded by Mexican lancers, 20 of them. They fired at him continuously. He was able to kill one. The rest came on and threw their lances at him. He was one of the last to be killed.

I could read no further. I removed myself to the living room, sat down in my chair by the fireplace, glanced at the fire, and wept.

Hardin was dead. Hardin, who fought in the Black Hawk War, who welcomed me to Springfield and joined the sessions by the fireplace in Speed's store, who served with me in the legislature, who was my rival for leadership in the Whig Party in Illinois, who saved me from risking my life against Shields, who brought Molly and me back together, who allowed raw ambition to separate us in the end, but who was my friend, was dead.

As a young man. I had known the pain of death—particularly those few close to me. Perhaps because I was older, though I grieved, this one haunted me. Why had Hardin died? Was there some purpose in it? Though dying bravely on the battlefield fighting for his country was heroic, it was a dreadful loss. If there were a purpose, it would take me time to discern it.

I returned to the details of my daily life, but Hardin's death was constantly in my thoughts. Poking its head through my grief, though, was an odd thought. I wasn't sure how I felt about it. With Hardin's death, the road was clearing for me to be the leader of the Whig Party in Illinois. Of course, there was Baker, but he had talked of moving to Galena, or even the West.

In October, 1847, a few weeks before we were to leave for Washington, I tidied up my outstanding cases. With two unfinished cases in Charleston, in Coles Country near the Indiana border, I decided to travel there. Another reason for making the trip was a case in Charleston that was attracting much attention. It concerned a family of runaway slaves. Because my Charleston cases were simple ones, I would have time to join either side in the trial.

The facts in the case were that Robert Matson, a Kentuckian from a wealthy family, owned large farms in both Kentucky and Illinois. Matson brought slaves with him to his Illinois farm in the spring and, in the late summer, returned with them to Kentucky. Each year he brought a different group. This was not against the law unless he domiciled them, which meant he kept them permanently at his Illinois home. Thinking their master intended to sell them into the deep South, a slave family ran off from Matson's Illinois farm.

Two abolitionists, Gideon Ashmore and Hiram Rutherford, were sheltering the family. Matson initiated legal action to regain the slaves and sued Ashmore and Rutherford for aiding their escape. The opposing counsels, Usher Linder for Matson and Orlando Ficklin for the slave family, had served in the legislature with me.

When I reached Charleston, Linder came immediately to my hotel and asked me to join him in representing the slaveholder Matson.

"Lincoln," he said, "There's more to this case than you know."

"What have you learned?" I asked.

"Matson employed a slave whom he had freed, Anthony Bryant, in Illinois as his overseer," he began. "The following year he brought Bryant's wife and their children to Illinois."

He paused for a moment before adding, "Now it gets a little complicated. Matson's housekeeper, with whom he was having an illicit relationship, grew jealous of Bryant's wife, and urged Matson to sell her and her children. This caused their flight to Ashmore's house. Do you follow?"

"I do," I replied.

"Lincoln, will you join me in representing Matson?"

"Well, Linder," I said, "since you are the first to ask me, I will."

"Well done," he exclaimed. "Can you meet with me tonight to prepare for tomorrow?"

"I will look forward to it," I answered.

On Saturday night, October 16, the proceedings took place in the Charleston courthouse. It was a square brick building with a cupola. The courthouse was in the town square, and the trial was the greatest event in Charleston in some years. A huge crowd, not all of whom could be admitted to the courtroom, surrounded the square. The proceedings consisted of presentation of evidence, the lawyer's statements, and the judge's decision. The verdict would be rendered that evening.

Representing the slave family, Ficklin spoke first. His major argument was that, by the terms of the Northwest Ordinance of 1787 and the Constitution of Illinois, Jane Bryant and her four children were free.

Charles Constable, Ficklin's associate, spoke next. He cited numerous English and American decisions in favor of the emancipation of slaves. Constable did concede that a slave owner had the right of *passage in situ* by which he could transport his slaves through free states, but if he domiciled the slaves in free territory for any length of time, the slaves became free.

Linder opened for us. He argued vehemently that slaves were a master's property. He cited the history of slavery in our country: that it existed well prior to the Declaration of Independence, that it existed in all 13 colonies, and that the Constitution protected slavery and contained a provision for the return of escaped slaves. Linder portrayed Matson as an extremely kind and indulgent slave owner who was entitled to the return of his property.

Finally, it was my turn.

I rose to address the court. Although I had now spoken on hundreds of occasions, it still took a minute or two for me to get my rhythm. When I began, my voice was high-pitched, my pace was quick, and my hands were in motion. I'm sure I looked awkward and ill-fitted for the task. I worked my way through this and settled in to my normal pace.

In presentation, I summarized our case.

"Gentlemen, this case turns on one simple question. What was Robert Matson's purpose in bringing his slaves to Illinois?

"To answer this question, we have to look first at his yearly practice. In the spring, he transported his slaves from his farm in Kentucky, over the Ohio River, to his farm in Illinois. In the fall he transported them back to Kentucky. These, gentlemen, were seasonal workers. This practice was not against the law of either the commonwealth of Kentucky or the state of Illinois.

"Robert Matson did not violate the law. His slaves violated the law when they ran off his farm. They are his property. If he wishes to sell them, that is his right.

"I will frankly admit that if Robert Matson brought his slaves to Illinois, and placed them on his farm permanently, he effected their emancipation.

"But why would Matson do that when he knew his slaves would gain their freedom?

"Those slaves are Robert Matson's property. To remove them from him without evidence of his intent to domicile them is to substitute sentiment for the cold, hard face of the law."

After the arguments, the judge withdrew to reach a decision. He had been deeply attentive; that much we knew. We waited anxiously for none of us had perceived a hint of how our arguments were being received. Each of us was expectant of a favorable result.

When he returned the judge declared, "Jane Bryant did not violate the law when she and her children fled from Robert Matson's farm believing they would be sold. When Robert Matson domiciled Jane Bryant and her children on his farm, by the law of the state of Illinois, he emancipated them. The prisoners shall be discharged and go free."

Not only did I lose the case, but before I could collect my fee, Matson fled back to Kentucky. As an experienced attorney, I still needed to learn whom to trust. In retrospect, I realized that Matson's case was weak. Nonetheless, he was entitled to legal representation that sought strenuously to win it for him.

On October 25, 1847, Molly, Bob, Eddie, and I left Springfield to travel to Washington, D.C., for the 30th Congress. The trip would take six weeks, but we planned to spend three weeks with Molly's family in Lexington, Kentucky. Though her father occasionally came to Springfield, she had not returned home for eight years.

We rented our house for ninety dollars per annum to Cornelius Ludlum. My departure was saluted in the *Illinois State Journal* on October 28. "Success to our talented member of Congress! He will find many men in Washington who possess twice the good looks, and not half the good sense, of our own representative."

After riding in a stage to Alton, we boarded a steamboat for St. Louis. Continuing to Cairo by steamboat, we changed to a river steamer, which took us up the Ohio River. We journeyed on to Frankfort, via the Kentucky River, and then by train to Lexington.

When we reached the Todd mansion in the center of town, the entire family stood on the steps to welcome us. I was acquainted with Molly's father, but not anyone else. With Molly's five brothers and sisters and eight more half sisters and brothers, our little family was but a drop in this ocean of relatives.

That evening, Molly's half sister, Emilee, who was 11, couldn't resist telling her what happened just as we arrived.

Emilee's cousin, Joseph Humphreys, happened to be on the train we took from Frankfort to Lexington. When Joseph arrived at the Todds before we did, he couldn't wait to tell his Aunt Eliza, Molly's stepmother, a ghastly tale about his train ride.

Emilee breathlessly repeated what Joseph told his aunt.

"I was never so glad to get off a train in my life. There were two lively youngsters on board who kept the whole train in turmoil, and their long-legged father, instead of spanking the brats, looked pleased as punch and aided and abetted the older one in mischief."

Emilee and Molly laughed heartily realizing that it was, of course, us. More squalls of laughter almost prevented Emilee from telling the second half of the story: the mortification of cousin Joseph upon our arrival!

We spent a delightful three weeks with Molly's family. We were warmly welcomed.

I sensed Mr. Todd took a liking to me in Springfield, and he was even more cordial in Lexington. We were both ardent Whigs, and he promised to introduce me to his friend Henry Clay.

He was making the arrangements for a speech Clay was to give in Lexington on November 13. At the age of 70, Clay was feeling his way into a fourth campaign for president. Mr. Todd invited me to accompany him to Clay's speech, which was to be the platform for his candidacy.

At the end of our visit, Mr. Todd gave us the deed to 80 acres of land in Springfield and pledged yearly gifts to Molly to supplement my income. He also asked me to represent him in his business affairs in Springfield.

Before we left for Washington, on a cold, gloomy November day, I heard Henry Clay speak to a massive crowd in Market Square. Mr. Todd and I sat together on the speaker's platform. I was 10 feet from the man I admired as my ideal politician, a man whose life in politics shaped our country.

I had never heard or seen anything so thrilling. Tall and thin like me, with the gray hair of wisdom, he rose to address the crowd. Aware that my own voice was high-pitched—as a listener, I welcomed the pitch and timbre of his voice. It was a baritone, mellower and more resonant than mine—alluring and enticing. It was almost as if we didn't need the words.

The words themselves were musical notes—a lush melody that warmed and relaxed the crowd. Just his voice brought him closer to the audience. Then came the animation of his face. As he turned toward the crowd in my direction, it expressed a friendly interest in each person present. "It is for you and to you, that I speak today," it seemed to say.

He opened with a disclaimer.

"I have come here with no purpose to attempt to make a fine speech, or any ambitious oratorical display. I have brought with me no rhetorical bouquets to throw into this assemblage. In the circle of the year, autumn has come, and the season of flowers has passed away. In the progress of years, my spring time has gone by, and I too am in the autumn of life, and feel the frost of age."

The heart of his speech was his position on the Mexican War. It was clear. The annexation of Texas started it.

"If we had not Texas, we should have no war," he declared.

President Polk had initiated the fighting. He gave General Taylor the order to move his army to the eastern shore of the Rio Grande. The Mexicans attacked to defend their country.

Eighteen months later, our armies occupied large amounts of Mexican territory. Some Democrats were calling for the conquest of the entire country. He proclaimed there should be no new territory added to our country from the Mexican War. If that were to happen, he foresaw a national calamity.

The death of his son in the Battle of Buena Vista might have caused his thoughts to turn to war itself.

"War is the voluntary work of our own hands, and whatever reproaches it may deserve should be directed to ourselves. When it breaks out, its duration is indefinite and unknown—its vicissitudes are hidden from our view. In the sacrifice of human life, and in the waste of human treasure in its losses and in its burthens, it affects both belligerent nations; and its sad effects of mangled bodies, of death, and of desolation, endure long after its thunders are hushed in peace. War unhinges society, disturbs its peaceful and regular industry, and scatters poisonous seeds of disease and immorality which continue to germinate and diffuse their baneful influence long after it has ceased. Dazzling by its glitter, pomp, and pageantry, it begets a spirit of wild adventure and romantic enterprise, and often disqualifies those who embark in it, after their return from the bloody fields of battle, from engaging in the industrious and peaceful vocations of life."

It was an oratorical masterpiece. I had never heard anyone speak more eloquently about the scourge of war. It had claimed the lives of Clay's son and my friend Hardin. What had been gained by the sacrifice of 25,000 American soldiers?: Territory that would enflame the controversy over slavery. Blood on the hands of President Polk that would not wash away.

When the program finished, the guests on the speaker's platform lingered to congratulate the presidential candidate. Mr. Todd led me toward Clay, and he waited his turn to introduce me.

When Clay pivoted toward him, he greeted Mr. Todd warmly.

"Todd, my good friend, how kind of you to make the arrangements for today."

Mr. Todd smiled, motioned toward me, and said, "I'd like to introduce my son-in-law, Mr. Abraham Lincoln."

Clay looked bewildered and said, "Abraham Lincoln? I don't know you. Should I know you?"

Mr. Todd replied, "He's just been elected to Congress from Illinois—the only Whig representative from the state."

Clay eyed me, said, "Congratulations, my boy. You'll do just fine," and turned away to talk to the other guests.

Chapter Twenty-One

This is The Slaves' Country Too

On the evening of December 2, Molly, our children, and I arrived at Union Station in Washington. We took a carriage to Brown's Hotel on Pennsylvania Avenue where we stayed for several days.

We all came to Washington with different perspectives. I hoped to learn about our national government, to support the Whig program, and to win recognition for myself. Molly wanted to support me and to participate in Washington's social life. Four-year-old Bobby came to have fun, while Eddie, at just 18 months, came to play with his brother.

Like Springfield, Washington was forging its identity. And, like Springfield, it had its share of hogs roaming the muddy streets. Pennsylvania Avenue, which connected the White House and the Capitol, was a sea of uneven cobblestones upon which carriages lurched and swayed like frigates on choppy waves. The streets of the city featured clumps of buildings followed by vast stretches of open space. The population was 40,000, including 8,000 free Negroes and 2,000 slaves.

We settled permanently into a room at Mrs. Ann Spriggs's boardinghouse on Carroll Row across the street from the Capitol. Hardin and Baker had stayed there during their congressional terms, and Baker recommended it because all the boarders were Whigs. It had acquired a reputation as "the abolition house," but, though I was against abolition, I was open to listening to arguments for it. Eight of my fellow Whig congressmen lived at Mrs. Spriggs's establishment.

Although our room was slightly smaller than the one at the Globe Tavern, it was agreeable. The furniture was simple but comfortable, the closet space was adequate, and the wood burning in the fireplace helped keep the drafty room warm. We had a lovely view of Capitol Park where we hoped the boys could play. Meals were served in the dining room, where Molly was often the only woman. The men, who ate heartily and sloppily, took care not to swear when Molly was present.

By far, the best known congressman living at our boardinghouse was Joshua Giddings, an abolitionist from Ohio. Giddings was a tall, strapping man with a stoop in his shoulders, a strong voice, and a look of determination. With wavy white hair and keen eyes, he had a formidable manner and was used to commanding attention. Giddings was known as "the Lion of Ashtabula" for the county in the western reserve where he had grown up. For some reason, he took an interest in me.

One night after dinner, when the others had left and Molly had retired upstairs to be with the children, Giddings engaged me in conversation.

"Lincoln," he said, "I think we get along because we have similar backgrounds. I grew up in three states, I worked on family farms until I was 17, and didn't go to school. I loved reading and educated myself. My mentor was Elisha Whittlesy, a congressman. I read law under him, began my own practice, and served a term in the Ohio legislature. Ten years later, I was elected to Whittlesy's congressional seat."

"Those are very close parallels," I remarked.

"Except for one major difference: your views on slavery."

I nodded and looked down at the table.

"Are you with the rest of your Kentucky brethren who support colonization?"

"That is a possible solution. Henry Clay favors it, and on our trip to Lexington, before we arrived here, I learned that my father-in-law Robert Todd does as well."

Giddings could hardly contain his contempt. He leaned forward and roared at me, "Paying the slaveholders for their 'property' and then shipping the slaves to Central America or back to Africa?"

I didn't back off and raised my voice in return, "It's supported by the American Colonization Society. James Madison was one of its recent presidents."

"Has it occurred to you or any of the other luminaries, that this is the slaves' country too?"

"Surely you don't believe the black man will ever be the social equal of the white man?"

"I know the black man is my equal in the sight of God and that the Declaration of Independence applies to him as well as to me. Let us set him free and accept him as our fellow countryman."

"The country is not ready for that. You will push us to the brink of war. That is the problem with you abolitionists."

"Lincoln, let's not destroy our friendship so quickly. Give me time, and I will make an abolitionist of you! I understand our positions on the Mexican War are similar. Perhaps we can direct our bile at President Polk."

"I hope to address the House on that subject," I replied.

"Excellent, I have heard you give a good speech. In the meantime, tomorrow is your first day as a congressman. Be sure to get a good night's rest."

He rose, smiled at me, and gave me a slap on the back. I responded with equal warmth, and we climbed the stairs to our rooms.

On December 6 at noon, the first session of the 30th Congress was called to order in the Hall of Representatives. Upon entering the Hall, I was awestruck for the first time in Washington. The elegant dome with a pattern of inlaid gold decoration was supported by marble columns with white capitals. A huge brass lantern hung from the dome. In the semicircular hall, the tight rows of mahogany desks stood atop a floor of alternating black-and-white marble tile. Facing us high above the Speaker's rostrum was a marble statue of Clio, the muse of history. To her right was a large statue of the American eagle. It was a setting in which history would be made.

There were 232 of us. Certainly the best known was former president John Quincy Adams from Massachusetts. He was the only president to serve in Congress after completing his presidential term. A good number of us were freshmen. Seats were assigned by lot, and mine was in the last row on the majority side. The acoustics were adequate, but I could hear reasonably well from my position in the back of the chamber.

I wrote Billy in December, "As you are all so anxious for me to distinguish myself, I have concluded to do so, before long." It was time to get started.

The subject that was most on the minds of everyone in Washington was the Mexican War. By the time I took my seat in Congress, with Winfield Scott's army having captured Mexico City, the fighting had ceased.

In early January, Congressman George Ashmun of Massachusetts offered an amendment to a bill lauding Zachary Taylor for his role in the war. The Ashmun amendment specified that the war was "unnecessarily and unconstitutionally begun by the President of the United States." I joined 84 other Whigs voting in favor of it.

To explain my vote on the Ashmun amendment, I decided to address the House on the issue of President Polk's contention, made in his annual message to Congress on December 7, 1847, that Mexico "involved the two countries in war by invading the territory of the state of Texas, striking the first blow, and shedding the blood of our own citizens on our own soil." Because it would be such an important step for me, I spent almost two weeks preparing my speech. While I expected a successful outcome, I could not say the same for my wife.

Sadly, in early January, Molly's ambition to be accepted into Washington society met with several setbacks.

The gala of New Year's Eve was a reception for General James Shields celebrating his bravery in battle in the Mexican War. There was to be an elaborate dinner at the Fuller Hotel. Senator Stephen A. Douglas and several of the Whigs who lived at Mrs. Spriggs's boardinghouse would attend. We were not invited. I tried to console Molly that it was probably my fault for causing Shields to challenge me to the duel.

The Whig Speaker of the House and Whig Senator Daniel Webster were also giving balls that week, but we were not invited to either of them. I had no idea why we were ignored other than my suspicion that, because we came from the West, we were seen as rustic outsiders.

On New Year's Day, we attended President Polk's
White House levee for senators and congressmen and
their wives. We were told that the tradition was to
arrive at noon "in full dress." Molly looked stunning
in her white silk ball gown. When we entered the front
hall of the White House we were engulfed with people we did not know. No one paid any attention to us.
Molly still hoped for some recognition as we proceeded to the reception line to meet the president and his
wife. Unfortunately, President Polk greeted Molly with
a cold glance and limply shook my hand. As we left, I
apologized again. What could we expect from someone whom I had attacked in the House by voting for
the Ashmun amendment?

At the House session of January 12, I rose to address
the members about the Mexican War. This was the
chance for me to establish myself as a rising politician.

I focused on the key issue. President Polk was lying
when he said the Mexicans started the war by invading
Texas. He knew better. He used the tension between the
United States and Mexico to start a war with the goal
of taking territory that Mexico refused to sell. Then, all
to the better, he blamed the war on Mexico.

I had no doubt the President was lying and that his
conscience was afflicting him. I hit my hand on the
podium and exclaimed, "He feels the blood of this war,
like the blood of Abel, crying to Heaven against him.
His mind, tasked beyond its power, is running hither
and thither, like some tortured creature, on a burning
surface, finding no position, on which it can settle down,
and be at ease. He knows not where he is. He is a bewildered, confounded, and miserably perplexed man."

I finished by asking what we could expect from the misguided and confused president as the war ended and the process of settling the terms of the peace began.

That night at dinner, Giddings stayed behind to talk to me.

"Lincoln," he bellowed at me, "I liked your speech today on the Mexican War."

"Thank you," I replied.

"But you spoke too quickly and your gestures were awkward. You looked like a windmill."

"I was worried about the one-hour time limit."

"If that was the problem, you should have rehearsed more carefully. Even Daniel Webster and Henry Clay rehearse endlessly."

"I was overconfident," I admitted. "I never found my pace and rhythm. I was nervous speaking to such an eminent audience—including you and John Quincy Adams."

"You showed promise. You'll get used to it," he said reassuringly, "but Lincoln, I thought you were a cautious man. I suspect it won't be well received at home."

"I really hadn't thought of that."

He yelled, "You hadn't thought of that?"

"Not really."

"I hadn't realized you were that foolish," he said with disappointment, "You are the only Whig from Illinois. Baker and Shields have become war heroes. Hardin lost his life fighting for his country. They are from your district. The Democrats will brand you a traitor and accuse you of stabbing your friends in the back. Some of the Whigs will agree with them. You will not be re-elected, and if Logan should run, he will lose."

"But you agreed with what I said in the speech," I protested.

"Yes—if that had been your purpose. It was obvious to everyone that you were trying to make a name for yourself."

With my head downcast, I said, "Well, it appears that I did."

At the end of January, a letter from Billy caused me consternation. He wrote it on January 19, a week after my House speech. Giddings was right. Billy reported many of my constituents were upset by my lack of support for the brave men from the district. While the strongest criticisms were coming from the Democrats, many Whigs were angry with me as well.

In mid-February, we learned the Mexican government agreed to terms to end the war. Mexico was forced to cede upper California, New Mexico, and Texas above the Rio Grande. For this, the US government was to pay $15,000,000. Most Whigs were unhappy with the agreement. We were concerned that the Democrats would push to extend slavery into the new territory. On March 10, the Senate ratified the treaty by a vote of 38–14. The focus would now turn to the future uses of this land rather than the process through which it was acquired.

As the winter continued, Molly grew restless and cross. I was gone most of the day and often late into the evening. The weather was cold and rainy, and the children could not play in the Capitol Park. Eddie was often sick with a cough, but Bob was rambunctious. Molly was confined to our small room with them. Because she was so ill-tempered, she was not popular with the other boarders. Occasionally, one of Mrs. Spriggs's slaves would watch over the children, and Molly could get out and go shopping.

One afternoon, I tried to help by taking Bobby to visit the Patent Office. Several blocks away, it was a grand three-story building that was still under construction. On the third floor were models of the inventions that had received patents. They were housed in glass cases that allowed us to see them closely. Bobby shared my interest in all the inventions.

"Papa, what is this one?" he asked.

"That one is called a telescope."

"What does it do?"

I pointed to the smaller end of the tube.

"If you look through it right there and point it at something, it will look closer and larger."

"Can you see everything?"

"Yes, Bobby, you can see the ships at sea, and the stars at night."

He looked up at me and said, "Oh, Papa, I love the stars. Can we see all of them?"

"We can see most of them."

"If we discover a new one, will they name it after us?"

"I think they might."

He turned away from me and looked back at the telescope.

"How does it work?"

"Do you see the two pieces of glass?"

"I do."

"The one at the end is bigger, and the one for your eye is smaller. Someone found that if you shape them just right, they can make things look bigger."

"Papa, can we see some other inventions?"

We spent the afternoon looking at a steam engine, the newest plow, the cotton gin, and the telegraph. I told Bobby about an invention I had in mind to help a stranded steamboat.

He was very excited and asked, "Papa, if you do it, can we come back and see it here?"

"I hope so. You can work on it with me when we get home," I said.

With the coming of spring, Molly wanted to leave Washington. She had not made a single friend. We decided it was best for her to take the children and travel to Lexington to be with her family. I would remain in Washington until the end of the first session in mid-August. Then I would go to Lexington, and we would all return to Springfield.

Chapter Twenty-Two
THE READINESS IS ALL

In late November, I traveled to Washington for the second session of the 30th Congress, which began on December 4. Molly, Bobby, and Eddie remained in Springfield. I returned to Mrs. Spriggs's boardinghouse where I lived by myself for the duration of the session. I participated actively in our supper discussions, and I also had more time to spend with my colleagues.

We knew that the main issue before this session of Congress would be slavery. Would it expand into the territory we had taken from Mexico?

One night, Giddings motioned for me to stay after dinner. When the others had left, he looked at me with his commanding presence.

He asked, "Do you remember when we talked about your speech on the Mexican War last January?"

"I do," I replied.

"Perhaps there is redemption," he said earnestly. He looked me in the eye and asked, "Will you join me in sponsoring a bill to emancipate the slaves in the District?"

I was nonplussed. How could he have assumed I would join him in sponsoring anything so radical?

Sensing my bewilderment, he said, "Didn't you and Stone declare in 1837 that Congress has the power to abolish slavery in the District of Columbia?"

"Yes, we did assert that, but we also said it should be exercised only at the request of the people in the District."

Giddings continued, "Since the federal government administers the District and the territories, do you believe slavery should be kept out of the territories?"

"Yes, I do."

"Do you believe that even though the slave trade continues, it is unconstitutional and must be ended?"

"Yes."

"You voted again and again for the Wilmot Proviso. Do you believe slavery should be kept out of any territory acquired by the Mexican War?

"Yes, I did. But what is the meaning of all this?"

"Lincoln, I am showing that you are an antislavery man, and you should join me in proposing that the slaves in the District be emancipated."

I scratched my head, leaned back, looked at him, and began to speak slowly.

"Let me answer you with a story:

"An old acquaintance of mine settled on a piece of barren prairie. It was a terrible, rough place to clear up, but after a while he got a few things growing—here and there a patch of corn, a few hills of beans, and so on. One day a stranger stopped to look at his place, and wanted to know how he managed to cultivate it. 'Well,' was the reply, 'some of it is pretty rough. The smaller stumps I can generally root out or burn out; but now and then there is a large old one that I can't, and there is no way but to plough around it.' Now, my friend, on the slavery issue, the only way to get along at all is to plough around it."

"Then what happens to that large old stump the farmer can't remove?"

"He lets it rot, and it falls of its own weight."

He paused, looked away, and then back at me as if he was absorbed in thought.

"So you won't join me in the fight to emancipate the slaves in the District?"

"Probably not."

"What is your reluctance?"

"I admire you and your passion to end slavery, but abolitionist doctrines are causing alarm in the South. They make compromise impossible. Slavery is tearing the country apart. It is best to proceed with patience, moderation, and caution. If I made a mistake with my opposition to the Mexican War, I do not want to repeat the mistake on the slavery issue."

He turned the conversation in another direction.

"You represented Matson in his attempt to recover his slaves."

"I did," I said clearly.

"How could you?"

"It was my duty as a lawyer."

"But I too am a lawyer, and I would never have taken that case. You had no moral objection to representing Matson?"

"I did not."

"Is there no moral issue for you in holding people in bondage?"

"You know that in 1837, Stone and I wrote that slavery was both an injustice and bad policy."

"You can be against slavery in the abstract, but when you take a step further, your outlook changes. You are no longer able to claim it is only an injustice. When you declare that no man has the right to own another, you understand that it is not only unjust—it is immoral."

"I will think about this, but I must say there is a time and a place for such things. I am not sure the time is now," I concluded.

Giddings pressed on, "Lincoln, do not misread me. I know how far you have come on the slavery issue. You were born among slaveholders and educated in the belief that slavery was just, proper, and necessary. You have been the only Whig representative from Illinois, surrounded at home by a proslavery sentiment little modified from that of Kentucky. You have worked to overcome this, and I am proud to stand with you as an antislavery man."

"Thank you, Giddings," I replied.

On the evening of Friday, January 14, Giddings and I returned to the boardinghouse from a late session in the House. We found the place in an uproar.

A distraught Mrs. Spriggs was trying to comfort Sylvia Wilson, a free negro who was one of the maids.

Giddings rushed to her and shouted, "Why, Mrs. Spriggs, whatever could have happened?"

"Oh, Mr. Giddings and Mr. Lincoln," she cried, "It is an abomination. The slave traders have seized Walter while he was waiting on the table."

"No," yelled Giddings, "Where have they taken him?"

"To the Williams Slave Pen where they plan to sell him tonight."

"This is barbarous and unconscionable, and I will not abide it," cried Giddings, although he knew there was very little he could do.

"Oh, Mr. Giddings, it is all that and more," she declared through her tears. "Walter and Sylvia were paying his owner $300 for his freedom. They were just $15 away. His owner has betrayed them and sold Walter to the slave traders for the full $300. "

"Heinous and treacherous," yelled Giddings, "Lincoln, can you have any doubt of this evil?"

"They burst in here, threatened us with pistols, and grabbed Walter," sobbed Mrs. Spriggs. She broke down weeping again as she held Sylvia in her arms.

After a few moments, she was able to continue. "One of them choked him by the neck while the others wrestled him down and handcuffed him. They aimed pistols at Walter and us, and they forced him out the door into a hack. All this in front of Sylvia who was protecting their child."

She let go of Sylvia who collapsed on the stairs.

When Giddings heard this, he rushed out into the night. I presumed he was on his way to the slave pen.

Over the next few days, I began to think differently about my experiences with slavery. At Farmington and at the Todd mansion in Lexington, I thought nothing of slaves routinely waiting on me. The image of the slaves chained together on the steamboat Speed and I took from Louisville to St. Louis began to haunt me. Perhaps their songs were songs of pain and sorrow and not carefree songs.

When I walked through Washington at night, I walked by the Franklin and Armfield Slave Pen, which was in view of the Capitol. Droves of negroes were brought there, temporarily kept, and finally taken to Southern markets, precisely like droves of horses.

I thought about the conversations I'd had with Speed about slavery. He had echoed his brother's view that the slaves at Farmington were treated humanely. It certainly wasn't true for most of the slaves in the South. Given the chance, wouldn't the Speeds' slaves prefer freedom to a life in bondage?

Several nights later, I walked down the hall and knocked on Giddings's door.

He welcomed me into his room, and we sat in the two chairs next to his small table.

"You are ready," he said.

"I am," I replied.

"What will you do?"

"I want to introduce a bill in the House emancipating the slaves in the District. I would like you to review the provisions with me."

"What are they?"

"First, the US Treasury will compensate an owner full cash value for any slave emancipated in the District."

He looked noncommittal, but asked me to continue.

"Second, all children of slave mothers on or after January 1, 1850, will be free."

"Yes," he said, "what is next?"

"Third, federal officials from slaveholding states on public business may be attended by necessary servants."

He did not look pleased, and said, "For 'necessary servants,' we read 'slaves?'"

"Yes."

"All right, what comes next?"

"Fourth, the municipal authorities are required to provide active and efficient means to arrest, and deliver up to their owners, all fugitive slaves escaping into the District."

"And the vote is last?"

"Yes, the provisions are enacted if the act is passed by the voters on the first Monday of April, 1849."

He took his time to reflect on what I had proposed, and then he said, "As you know I am against compensated emancipation, but your proposal is sensible, and it may be the best we can get at this time. Over the next few days, we will meet with Mayor Seaton and as many influential people as we can. If we can win their support, I believe we can pass your bill."

"I will do my best," I told him, and then added, "Is there any news of Walter?"

"There is," he said. "The slave traders lied to me. They said he was taken to Alexandria and shipped to New Orleans. That was a lie. He is still in their pen, and I am engaged in a legal struggle with the traders and the owner. Since they know I really don't have recourse to the law, it is mostly by threat, but it seems to be working. We may be able to buy him back, but the price, at present, is exorbitant. If we can lower it, will you contribute?"

"Of course," I said, "and so will many of the Whigs in the House."

On January 10, I presented my proposal to the House to emancipate the slaves in the District of Columbia.

I read the provisions of the proposal, and then added that I was authorized to say the proposition had been submitted to 15 of the leading citizens of the District, and all were in favor.

When I made this announcement, I was greeted with cries of, "Who are they? Give us their names."

I did not identify any of them.

Within hours, however, the Southern members of Congress learned the name of each one. During that evening and the next day, they descended on them like jackals. Mayor Seaton, whose support had been wobbly, was the first to collapse. The others followed.

The next day, I withdrew my bill knowing that further effort was useless.

With this defeat, my career in Congress came to a close. For a few more weeks, I attended each day, but very little business was conducted. Adjournment came on March 3, 1849.

The night before I was to leave for home in late April, I paid a farewell visit to Giddings. I learned the good news that Walter had been freed and returned to his family. I thanked Giddings for his counsel and friendship.

"I believe you will return to Washington," he said, "and I look forward to seeing you again."

On the long journey home, by train to Chicago and then coach to Springfield, I reflected on my life. Much like my long walks through the woods in New Salem, the train trip brought the solace I needed to retreat into my thoughts. As the engine pulled out of Washington, I pondered my experience in Congress.

In January 1848, after I had served in the House for a month, Billy wrote that my reelection was already desired. Logan was not included in our original rotation agreement, so I didn't have to yield the seat for him. Whig leaders in the seventh district also realized he would be a weak candidate. Just months later, the reelection opportunity was gone. How had that happened?

I voted for the Ashmun amendment, but so did 84 other Whigs. Before I'd gained enough experience, and anxious to make a name for myself, I let ambition get the better of me. I tried to distinguish myself with my speech on the Mexican War, but it backfired. Some of the speech was really an elevated slasher-gaff attack on President Polk. My political instincts deserted me. I spoke for what I thought was right, but it was not welcomed in the seventh district. Billy reported I was becoming unpopular. I had brought it on myself.

It hurt all the more because in the second session, without the distraction of Molly and the children, I began to understand how the political process worked in the House. I needed a mentor like Joshua Giddings to teach me, but it was too late.

It was impossible not to compare myself to Stephen Douglas. How swiftly he rose from the Illinois Supreme Court to the House of Representatives and then to the Senate. His colleagues were now John C. Calhoun, Daniel Webster, Jefferson Davis, Hannibal Hamlin, and Sam Houston. He was becoming a leader in the Democratic Party and, although young, a possible presidential candidate. I was finished after one term in the House.

I was not a success in the pursuit I loved. My political career was over.

I lay back in the seat and fell asleep.

When I awoke we were passing through the green woods and mountains of Pennsylvania. The rhythm of the train moving steadily forward on the tracks eased me back into retrospection.

Twelve years earlier, I rode from New Salem to Springfield on the back of a borrowed horse. Now I was riding an iron horse across a thousand miles on iron rails. Before long we would be able to send written messages between Springfield and Washington in minutes. The system of internal improvements Henry Clay visualized for America—and which others and I strove to enact in legislatures around the country—was being created. The economic failure that doomed it temporarily was over. My country and I had grown up together.

In 1837, I journeyed to Springfield doubting myself and unsure of my ability to practice law. Now I was respected as one of the best lawyers in the state.

In my second term in the state legislature, I was still maturing as a politician; in 1849, as a representative in the US Congress, I introduced a bill abolishing slavery in the District of Columbia.

I came to Springfield in debt, with worldly possessions that fit into a saddlebag, and unsure if any young woman could take an interest in me. Twelve years later, I had no debt, owned a house in Springfield, had married Mary Todd, and was the father of two boys.

When I arrived in Springfield, I was adept at the arts of the slasher-gaff and writing anonymous letters. I enjoyed the power to hurt. After 12 years, through the persistence of my friend Speed and my involvement in the scrape with Shields, I finally saw the power to hurt for what it was.

We crossed Pennsylvania on into Ohio and Indiana— the land of the Northwest Ordinance of 1787.

My thoughts began to turn toward Springfield.

I had my family and my law practice. To them I would dedicate myself.

I felt my friendship with Speed receding. It was the last burst of youth that brought us together. My growing disgust with slavery was at odds with his support of it.

In 1849, I turned 40 years old.

Molly was now my companion, and the children were the joy of our lives.

As I traveled in the coach from Chicago to Springfield, I sat by myself.

We drew closer to my home, and I looked out the window. It was a lovely April day. Spring was always my favorite time of year in Illinois. A flock of meadowlarks, their yellow breasts shining in the morning sun, hovered above the returning green of the prairie. They rose upward with sharp, rapid wing beats and then glided away toward the horizon.

I would always be a man of the prairie.

The prairie called to me in all its fullness. Under a luminous blue sky, the radiant green grass swept out toward the deeper green of the distant oak trees. Early sunflowers, blue sage, and the white blossoms of the old plainsman swayed in the gentle breeze. Large cumulus clouds floated away to the east.

It continued to speak of possibilities, but all I could see was limits: purpose was lost, ambition crushed.

Do not despair, it called. Your time may come. The readiness is all.

ACKNOWLEDGMENTS

When I started writing a sequel to *Young Lincoln*, Josh Stevens, the founder of Reedy Press, warned me that the book must stand on its own. I believe it does, and I believe you will find *Lincoln in Springfield* a very different book from *Young Lincoln*. Lincoln's growth is two steps forward and one step back. The steps back may disappoint us, but they are an essential part of the story.

To Josh, I owe my thanks for his vision and guidance. Reedy Press is one of St. Louis's jewels, and I am honored to be a Reedy author.

In the revisions that are the heart of the writing process, Kathleen Dragan, my editor at Reedy Press, became a partner in shaping and deepening the story. Kathleen's sense of the manuscript's potential and her attention to detail guided us through the six months of editing.

I am blessed to have three giants of Lincoln Studies as my friends. To Bob Bray, Michael Burlingame, and Doug Wilson, I owe my growing understanding of Lincoln.

The responses from the young adult readers of Young Lincoln showed me that Abe's story resonates with today's teenagers. At a signing at the Lincoln Home, one young fellow asked me, "Will there be a sequel?" When I replied, "Hopefully several," he beamed and said, "Ooh! It will be the Harry Potter of Abraham Lincoln." To all my young friends who wrote me e-mail, I give my deepest thanks. The greatest joy in writing is to hear from a reader.

My thanks to Sarah LaPierre (Wydown Middle School in St. Louis), Bella Barclay (Healdsburg JHS in Healdsburg, CA), and Robert Donahue (Dexter Southfield School in Boston) who had their classes read *Young Lincoln* and invited me to meet with their students. What a privilege! Sarah invited me to share the manuscript of *Lincoln in Springfield* with her class, but Covid intervened. Anyone who believes that the youth of America is being corrupted by video games and social media needs to join me on one of these visits.

Teaching lifelong learners in the Washington University OLLI program has been a highlight of this journey. For the invitation to participate, I thank Katie Compton, the director.

Independent bookstores are an author's lifeblood. My thanks to Kelly Von Plonski, Alex Weir, and Gena Brady at Subterranean Books in St. Louis; Dave Mull and Christy Blackwell at the Lincoln Home Shop; and B. J. Euler and Dorothy Happe-Shelton at the Gift Shop in New Salem. I appreciate their kindness and their interest in me and my writing.

My wife Ginger has been my north star for almost 40 years. Our journey together has been joyful and blessed. For loving and supporting me, I am eternally grateful to her.

AUTHOR SOURCE NOTES

This is a work of fiction.

In writing it, I have tried to remain true to the historical record. My hope is to interest young adult readers in Lincoln's life and times. I owe them a story that is grounded in the truth, but at the heart of which is the premise that Lincoln can tell us what he is thinking and feeling. That's the fictional element in both *Young Lincoln* and *Lincoln in Springfield*.

There are many excellent biographies and histories of Lincoln's life. I have relied on many of them. I've tried to find the most reliable stories about Lincoln and his life in Springfield from 1837 to 1849 and to adapt them to the form of a young adult historical novel. So, is it a novel or a biography? My friend Bob Bray calls it "novelography," and I'll take that.

This is also to say that "my poor power to add or detract" is indebted to the work of scholars in the field of Lincoln Studies. In the notes that follow, you will see how much they have contributed to the story. I am deeply grateful to all of them.

There are three sources upon which I have relied most heavily. Michael Burlingame's biography, *Abraham Lincoln: A Life* has been my Bible. James McPherson has said that "Michael Burlingame knows more about Lincoln than anyone living." What a resource this is for those of us who write about Lincoln. Douglas Wilson's award-winning book, *Honor's Voice* (1999), has guided my thinking about Lincoln's courtship and marriage.

In this book, I have used Lincoln's words from *The Collected Works* (ed. by Roy P. Basler) more liberally than I did in *Young Lincoln*. The notes indicate the places in the text where Abe's words are his own and not mine.

In *Lincoln in Springfield*, I have used a number of primary sources: newspapers, letters, documents, legal papers, and, of course, *The Collected Works*. I've learned to make my way around the internet, and my thanks to all the librarians and friends who have made that possible.

Sources

Abbreviations and Short titles employed in notes:

Burlingame, *AL: A Life:* Michael Burlingame, *Abraham Lincoln: A Life, Volume One* (Baltimore: Johns Hopkins University Press, 2008).

CW: Roy P. Basler, ed., *The Collected Works of Abraham Lincoln*, 9 vols., (New Brunswick, NJ: Rutgers University Press, 1953–55).

HI: Douglas L. Wilson and Rodney O. Davis, eds., *Herndon's Informants: Letters, Interviews, and Statements about Abraham Lincoln* (Urbana: University of Illinois Press, 1998).

Preface
vii "By the way …" CW, 1:260.

Chapter 1
5 "He strutted around …" Robert Taft, "The Appearance and Personality of Stephen A. Douglas," *Kansas Historical Quarterly* (Topeka: Kansas Historical Society), Spring 1954, 9–14.

7 "No, he asked me to give him credit …" Joshua F. Speed, *Reminiscences of Abraham Lincoln* (Forgotten Books, 2012) 21.

7 'Well, Speed,' he said, 'I am moved.' Speed, *Reminiscences*, 22.

7 "I was there when Forquer said …" Speed, *Reminiscences*, 17.

8 "He's drunk and been beating his wife." Burlingame, *AL: A Life*, 104–105.

Chapter 3

22 The county courthouse presided ... Paul M. Angle, *"Here I Have Lived": A History of Lincoln's Springfield* (New Brunswick, NJ: Rutgers University Press 1935), 43.

22 Above all, I would be honest ... Daniel Stowell, ed., *Papers of Abraham Lincoln: Legal Documents and Cases, Volume One*, (Charlottesville: University of Virginia Press, 2008), 13.

23 "Chicken Row" Angle, *Here I Have Lived*, 44

24 He led me into the office ... Bryan Andreason, *Lincoln's Springfield* (Carbondale: Southern Illinois University, 2015), 44–45.

25 ... I kept a surplus of $16. Burlingame, *AL: A Life*, 78.

26 "There's this fellow ..." Burlingame, *AL: A Life*, 132.

27 "It seems that last fall, this fellow ..." Stowell, *Papers of Abraham Lincoln, Volume One*, 27–29.

28 "Light sorrel horse ..." Stowell, *Papers of Abraham Lincoln, Volume One*, 28.

29 "My husband owned 10 acres of land ..." Burlingame, *AL: A Life*, 133–136.

31 "... he defended Nathan Van Noy." Sangamon County Historical Society: sangamoncountyhistory.org/wp/?p=2731

Chapter 4

34 To calm the town ... Richard Lawrence Miller, *Lincoln and His World: Prairie Politician: 1834–1842* (Mechanicsburg, PA: Stackpole Books, 2008), 162–163.

41 'Gentlemen, have you no other champion ...' Burlingame, *AL: A Life*, 138.

42 "The recent noise and excitement ..." Burlingame, *AL: A Life*, 135.

Chapter 5

46 "You know then that my players …" Angle, *"Here I Have Lived*, 100.

46 "No sooner was construction …" Joseph Jefferson, *The Autobiography of Joseph Jefferson* (New York: The Century Co., 1889), 30.

48 "He regaled me …" Jefferson, *The Autobiography*, 25.

50 "It's for the footlights …" Jefferson, *The Autobiography*, 29.

Chapter 6

56 During the trial, I was constantly interrupted … John J. Duff, *A. Lincoln: Prairie Lawyer* (New York: Rinehart and Company, 1960), 40.

56 Our client, Wooldridge … Jesse W. Weik, *The Real Lincoln: A Portrait* (Lincoln: University of Nebraska Press, 2002), 134–138.

56 "struck, beat, bruised …" Burlingame, *AL: A Life*, 132.

57 One of the suits … Burlingame, *AL: A Life*, 132.

59 "In March, we filed a statement …" Burlingame, *AL: A Life*, 122.

59 "As you may know, I was a student …" William H. Herndon and Jesse W. Weik, *Herndon's Lincoln* (Urbana: University of Illinois Press, 2006), 125.

61 "I will hire McDougall …" Burlingame, *AL: A Life*, 132.

61 "Whatever spiteful fools …" Herndon and Weik, *Herndon's Lincoln*, 126.

63 I began by reflecting on our republic in the year 1837. CW, 1:108.

Chapter 7

71 "In Hancock County ..." Erika Holst, *Wicked Springfield* (Charleston: The History Press, 2010), 16.

72 "my private and moral ..." Burlingame, *AL: A Life*, 139.

72 "Isn't that the best way ..." CW, 1:107.

73 "He bought himself a cane ..." Burlingame, *AL: A Life*, 142.

73 "If we do our duty ..." CW, 1:250.

79 There was a report ... Miller, *Lincoln and His World*, 257.

80 On September 29 ... Miller, *Lincoln and His World*, 259.

Chapter 8

83 "At 8:00 p.m. on the evening ..." Holst, *Wicked Springfield*, 22.

84 "He was engrossed ..." Miller, *Lincoln and His World*, 228–229.

84 "He continued his stream ..." Holst, *Wicked Springfield*, 24.

86 To take my mind off my task ... Andreason, *Lincoln's Springfield*, 52–53.

90 "Next, in a declaration given shortly before his death ..." Duff, *A. Lincoln: Prairie Lawyer*, 56.

Chapter 9

99 When Baker started to speak ... Herndon and Weik, *Herndon's Lincoln*, 129–130.

99 "wherever there is a land office ..." Herndon and Weik, *Herndon's Lincoln*, 129.

99 "And no man shall take him ..." Herndon and Weik, *Herndon's Lincoln*, 129.

100 "TO MAKE THE NEGRO ..." Burlingame, *AL: A Life*, 154.

101 He grabbed the book ... Burlingame, *AL: A Life*, 155.

101 "Any man who would write ..." Willard L. King, *Lincoln's Manager: David Davis* (Cambridge: Harvard University Press, 1960), 38.

101 Several weeks later ... James H. Matheny to WHH (interview), 1865–66, HI, 472.

102 "When the ox trod ..." *Aesop's Fables* (New York: New American Library [Signet Classics], 1992), 45.

103 And then I did something ... Herndon and Weik, *Herndon's Lincoln*, 130.

Chapter 10

108 Eventually, we were dubbed ... Stacy Pratt McDermott, *Mary Todd: Southern Girl, Northern Woman* (New York: Routledge, 2015), 38.

109 Conkling said I looked like ... Ronald C. White, Jr., *A. Lincoln* (New York: Random House, 2009), 110.

111 The favored place ... Holst, *Wicked Springfield*, 59–60.

112 "Our Irish blacksmith ..." CW, 1:184.

114 Mary had been in school ... McDermott, *Mary Todd*, 24.

115 "very creature of excitement" McDermott, *Mary Todd*, 41.

115 her lower half caked in mud ... McDermott, *Mary Todd*, 42.

115 "As I walked out ..." McDermott, *Mary Todd*, 42.

116 "Yet oft-times ..." Douglas Wilson, *Honor's Voice* (New York: Knopf, 1999), 190.

117 Spencer Turner was charged ... Duff, *A. Lincoln: Prairie Lawyer*, 70–71.

117 "and my hand will never be given ..." McDermott, *Mary Todd*, 40–41.

118 ... I had written to Eliza Browning ... CW, 1:119.

Chapter 11

123 ... she was known for her gentle temperament ... Burlingame, *AL: A Life*, 181.

123 "A lovelier girl I have never seen." McDermott, *Mary Todd*, 164.

125 'Making Augur Holes with a Gimlet' *Sangamo Journal*, November 13, 1840, 1.

Chapter 12

133 "I have written her a letter. I have it here." Joshua F. Speed (WHH interview), 1865–66, HI, 477.

133 "Speed, I have never known ..." Joshua F. Speed (WHH interview), 1865–66, HI, 477.

133 "Words are passed by ..." Joshua F. Speed (WHH interview), 1865–66, HI, 477.

135 I removed myself ... Observation about Lincoln made by Shelby Foote in Ken Burns's documentary, *The Civil War* Episode 1.

140 "Woe is me." Joshua F. Speed (WHH interview), 1865–66, HI, 475.

140 "Mr. Lincoln ... if you desire it ..." Elizabeth Todd Edwards (WHH interview), 1865–66, HI, 444.

Chapter 13

144 In November, I was elected … Joshua Wolf Shenk, *Lincoln's Melancholy* (Boston: Houghton Mifflin Company, 2005), 48–65.

147 I saw that Speed … Joshua F. Speed (WHH interview), 1865–66, HI, 475.

148 "Lincoln, you must rally or you will die." CW, 1:229.

148 'I am not afraid of death…' Speed, *Reminiscences*, 39.

148 He was a political colleague … Shenk, *Lincoln's Melancholy*, 57.

149 Once he made the diagnosis … Shenk, *Lincoln's Melancholy*, 58–59.

150 Stuart urged me to accept … Burlingame, *AL: A Life*, 184.

151 Rather than facing trial … Burlingame, *AL: A Life*, 135.

152 "I will ask Ninian and Elizabeth if we can take Julia." Richard E. Hart, *Circuses in Lincoln's Springfield* (Springfield: Spring Creek Series, 2013), 2.

152 With a fanfare from the band … Hart, *Circuses*, 22.

154 A pretty young woman trotted out … Hart, *Circuses*, 4.

154 Shortly thereafter, the showman disappeared … Hart, *Circuses*, 4.

Chapter 14

158 Walking home from one … Wilson, *Honor's Voice*, 185.

159 When I settled in at Butler's … Sarah Rickard Barrett to WHH (letter), August 3, 1888, HI, 663–664.

160 There I detailed the confusing history … Stowell, *Papers of Abraham Lincoln, Volume One*, 33.

160 ... the court erred in instructing ... Stowell, *Papers of Abraham Lincoln, Volume One,*, 33.

161 ... for seizing a horse and converting it to his own use. Stowell, *Papers of Abraham Lincoln, Volume One,*, 38–39.

162 "... with instructions to award a venire de novo." Stowell, *Papers of Abraham Lincoln, Volume One*, 39.

163 I told Butler's wife that it would just kill me to marry her. Burlingame, *AL: A Life*

165 My day at Farmington ... Shenk, *Lincoln's Melancholy*, 63.

167 from committing assault and battery on me. CW, 1:259–260.

167 "I seem to have taken more than my share." Burlingame, *AL: A Life*, 187.

168 "My dear boy, nothing could please me more!" Wilson, *Honor's Voice*, 250.

169 ... take it according to the truth. CW, 1:261.

169 One night, when Speed and I ... CW, 1:260.

Chapter 15

173 ... the pursuit of something ... Wilson, *Honor's Voice*, 246–247.

174 "... your brother William." CW, 1:265.

174 "... I have reasoned myself into a false position." Wilson, *Honor's Voice*, 252.

174 ... rather than 20 others ... CW, 1:266.

175 Reluctantly, I decided to go to the dentist. Andreason, *Lincoln's Springfield*, 14–15.

176 I immediately ceased my labors CW, 1:267–268.

177 Sitting by the fire at Butler's ... CW, 1:269–270.

177 I opened it with intense anxiety CW, 1:280

178 I welcomed his news ... CW, 1:280

Chapter 16

180 I wrote him that I was pleased to be thanked …
CW, 1:289.

181 While the letter was not unkind to Shields …
Wilson, *Honor's Voice*, 266–267.

182 I dashed the letter off in an afternoon. CW, 1:292–297.

183 In it, Shields wrote in part: Wilson, *Honor's Voice*, 275.

184 … unless Shields withdrew the first note. Wilson,
Honor's Voice, 276.

184 … I could not be degraded … Burlingame, *AL: A
Life*, 190.

185 … Shields withdraw the challenge first … Burlingame,
AL: A Life, 191.

186 "… 'Victory or Be Crippled.'" Burlingame, *AL:
A Life*, 192.

188 "… After Dr. Thomas Hope …" Burlingame, *AL:
A Life*, 193.

188 "… and no cause for any." CW, 1:301.

189 "A bowman took aim at an eagle …" *Aesop's Fables*, 157.

Chapter 17

192 "Ye jews-harps awake …" McDermott, *Mary Todd*, 49.

195 … to hug it all the more. Wilson, *Honor's Voice*, 288–291.

195 Please answer it quickly … CW, 1:303.

196 "… in each other's keeping." Burlingame, *AL:
A Life*, 195.

196 "To hell, I reckon." Wilson, *Honor's Voice*, 292.

196 … I was going to the slaughter … James H.
Matheny (WHH interview, May 3, 1866), HI, 251.

197 … an occasional raised eyebrow. Burlingame, *AL: A
Life*, 195.

197 At this, Judge Browne blurted … Burlingame, *AL: A Life*, 195–196.

198 "… a matter of profound wonder." CW, 1:305.

Chapter 18

204 Molly and I adapted … McDermott, *Mary Todd*, 36–37.

207 "Jim, I am now …" James H. Matheny (WHH interview, May 3, 1866), HI, 251.

Chapter 19

212 There were, however, times … Jean H. Baker, *Mary Todd Lincoln* (New York: W. W. Norton & Company, 2008), 106–107.

219 Hardin volunteered … Benjamin P. Thomas, *Abraham Lincoln* (New York: Barnes and Noble,1994), 107.

220 He is trying to turn … Burlingame, *AL: A Life*, 238.

221 "… and scoffer at, religion." CW, 1:382.

221 "… has not pleased me as much as I expected." CW, 1:390.

Chapter 20

227 "… He is ahead of me in the race of ambition." CW, 2:382–383.

228 At Buena Vista, Taylor's army… Chris DeRose, *Congressman Lincoln* (New York: Threshold, 2013), 63.

229 He was one of the last to be killed. DeRose, *Congressman Lincoln*, 63.

232 The courthouse was in the town square … Duff, *A. Lincoln: Prairie Lawyer*, 137.

233 These, gentlemen, were seasonal workers. Duff, *A. Lincoln: Prairie Lawyer*, 139.

233 … he effected their emancipation. Stowell, *Papers of Abraham Lincoln, Volume Two*, 33.

234 "… The prisoners shall be discharged and go free." Stowell, *Papers of Abraham Lincoln, Volume Two*, 33.

234 "… of our own representative." White, Jr., *A. Lincoln*, 139.

235 "… aided and abetted the older one in mischief." Burlingame, *AL: A Life*, 254.

236 The words themselves were musical notes … David S. Heidler and Jeanne T. Heidler, *Henry Clay: The Essential American* (New York: Random House, 2010), 30.

237 "War is the voluntary work of our own hands …" Henry Clay, Market Speech, November 13, 1847, Lexington, KY. henryclay.org/wp-content/uploads/2016/02/Market-Speech.pdf

Chapter 21

242 Although our room was slightly smaller … Daniel Mark Epstein, *The Lincolns: Portrait of a Marriage* (New York: Ballantine Books, 2008), 122.

244 "… Robert Todd does as well." David S. Reynolds, *Abe: Abraham Lincoln and His Times* (New York: Penguin Press, 2020), 162.

245 On December 6 at noon … Epstein, *The Lincolns*, 114.

245 I wrote Billy in December … CW, 1:420.

246 "… involved the two countries …" James Knox Polk, Third Annual Message to Congress, December 7, 1847, UVA Miller Center. millercenter.org/the-presidency/presidential-speeches/december-7-1847-third-annual-message

246 Sadly, in early January … Epstein, *The Lincolns*, 122–123.

247 "He feels the blood of this war…" CW, 1:439.

250 "Papa, what is this one?" Epstein, *The Lincolns*, 124.

Chapter 22

255 "An old acquaintance..." P. M. Zall, *Abe Lincoln Laughing* (Knoxville: University of Tennessee Press, 1995), 74.

257 You were born among slaveholders... DeRose, *Congressman Lincoln*, 230.

257 On the evening of Friday, January 14... DeRose, *Congressman Lincoln*, 112.

258 When I walked through Washington at night... CW, 2:253.

260 I read the provisions of the proposal... CW, 2:22.